D1467753

THE Aftermath OF THE Chinese Nationalist Revolution

KATHLYN GAY

 TWENTY-FIRST CENTURY BOOKS MINNEAPOLIS

Consultant: John Delury, PhD Chinese history and visiting assistant professor, Brown University

The image on the jacket and the cover is of a group of armed Chinese soldiers at Swatow (Shantou) on the first day of the outbreak of the Chinese Nationalist Revolution, January 1912. (Photo by Topical Press Agency/Getty Images).

Twenty-First Century Books
A division of Lerner Publishing Group, Inc.
241 First Avenue North
Minneapolis, MN 55401 U.S.A.

Website address: www.lernerbooks.com

Library of Congress Cataloging-in-Publication Data

Gay, Kathlyn.
    The aftermath of the Chinese nationalist revolution / by Kathlyn Gay.
        p.   cm. — (Aftermath of History)
        Includes bibliographical references and index.
        ISBN 978-0-8225-7601-3 (lib. bdg. : alk. paper)
        1. China—History—Republic, 1912–1949—Juvenile literature. 2. Revolutions—China—History—20th century—Juvenile literature. I. Title.
    DS774.G39 2009
    951.04—dc22   2007015082

Manufactured in the United States of America
1 2 3 4 5 6 – BP – 14 13 12 11 10 09

Contents

Introduction: A Bomb!   4

Chapter 1: Revolts across China   8

Chapter 2: Chaos after the Revolution   25

Chapter 3: The Struggle to Unify China   39

Chapter 4: Civil War   53

Chapter 5: War with Japan   67

Chapter 6: China in World War II   83

Chapter 7: The Rise of the "New China"   101

Epilogue   117

Timeline   122

Glossary   125

Who's Who?   127

Source Notes   138

Bibliography   146

For Further Reading and Websites   150

Index   152

A Bomb!

ON AN AUGUST AFTERNOON in 1911, angry students marched in the streets of Sichuan Province (similar to a state) in south central China. The students were protesting the imperial Manchu government's takeover of the railroads. Business people and wealthy investors, who stood to lose money because of the takeover, joined in. The military tried to break up the protests, killing thirty-two people.

The attempt to take over, or nationalize, the railroads was just one of many grievances against the imperial government. Anger at the government took a violent turn less than two months later. On October 10, 1911, a bomb exploded in the city of Wuchang in east central China. Police rushed to the scene, which turned out to be the headquarters of a secret organization called the "New Army" of China. Members of the group had accidentally set off the bomb that led to their discovery. They had been planning to overthrow the ruling Manchu family, who governed the Qing dynasty (line of rulers).

Like many Chinese citizens, members of the New Army opposed the Manchu rulers. The Manchu had long been viewed by their Chinese subjects as outsiders. They had invaded China in the 1600s from their native Manchuria. Their rule, which began in 1644, had problems from the start. The problems stemmed from the fact that they were from a different ethnic group with a different culture and language than the majority of Chinese subjects.

One of the touchiest subjects from more recent times involved the ruling family's dealings with outsiders. Since the 1840s, the Manchu had ceded control of China's foreign trade and even some of its territory to other countries. In the Opium War with Great Britain (1839–1842), in which China was defeated, the Manchu rulers signed the Treaty of Nanjing. The treaty gave Great Britain the right to open Chinese ports to foreign trade and to set taxes on goods coming into the country. The treaty also gave the island of Hong Kong to the British.

Other countries pressured China for the same kind of trading rights that the British had been granted. Again, the ruling Manchu family agreed to the terms set by foreign powers, signing a series of agreements that came to be known as the "unequal treaties." By the end of the 1800s, Austria, France, Germany, Great Britain, Italy, Japan, and Russia had all set up spheres of influence, or territories that they controlled, within China. Within these regions, each country claimed the exclusive right to trade or invest and to set and collect taxes on goods brought into China.

By the early 1900s, Sun Yat-sen, who would become a major revolutionary leader in China, observed that his country had become "the poorest and weakest nation in the world." He wrote, "We occupy the lowest position in international affairs. Other men are the carving knife and serving dish; we are the fish and the meat."

In addition to giving up control over Chinese trade and territory, the Manchu government had ignored growing social problems. Opium addiction, gambling, and infanticide (killing infants) threatened the health and well-being of China's 450 million people. Financial concerns also troubled the Chinese people. Grumblings

BY THE EARLY 1900S, SUN YAT-SEN HAD BECOME A MAJOR REVOLUTIONARY FIGURE IN CHINA.

and rumblings of discontent could be heard in many parts of China. Taxes were rising for the wealthy. Crops had failed. Floods added to the misery. Intellectuals, students, and business people wanted a change in government. They wanted to replace the ruling dynasty with a republican form of government, in which citizens choose who will represent them in the government.

After the October 10 explosion in Wuchang, the New Army quickly moved ahead with its planned revolt. That revolt sparked a revolution, the Chinese Nationalist Revolution, that would end Manchu rule. The revolution, which lasted only four months, would have lasting effects on China. In the aftermath of the revolution, China would experience years of chaos, conflict, and a destructive, years-long struggle for power and the right to govern China.

CHAPTER 1

Revolts across China

THE REVOLT BEGAN on October 10, 1911, shortly after the bomb blast. Encountering little resistance, the New Army seized control of a government weapons storehouse in Wuchang. Its members also attacked military offices, forcing commanders to flee. The Manchu rulers sent soldiers to crush the rebellion, but many imperial soldiers joined the rebel forces, and by noon of October 11, 1911, the New Army had control of Wuchang. Then they quickly took over the nearby cities of Hankou and Hanyang and established Nanjing (or Nanking) as their capital.

Word of the New Army's victory spread rapidly. The seizure of Wuchang and occupation of the other cities triggered revolts in villages and towns across southwest China. These revolts marked the beginning of the end of the Manchu ruling family's hold on China. From late October through November 1911, one province after another seceded (withdrew) from the empire. Two-thirds of China—fifteen provinces—declared independence and openly rebelled against China's capital city Peking (now called Beijing). Militias (citizen armies), which included angry peasants who had endured brutal treatment by imperial officials, rioted. They destroyed police stations and freed prisoners in jails, cut telegraph lines, and looted warehouses for weapons. They massacred Manchu soldiers in military posts.

In cities such as Guangzhou (Canton) and Shanghai, revolutionary fervor grew but did not always involve actual fighting. The fervor sometimes was reflected in theatrical productions, a popular form of Chinese entertainment. One play performed in Shanghai around this time, for example, was a tale about heroic revolutionary soldiers. A French traveler and writer who attended a performance describes one scene:

> The revolutionary soldiers charged a fortress, chasing from it the Manchus. . . . One could hear the fusillade [firearms] on all sides, and see a fire break out. Surprisingly, the fire did not overtake the new theater's many settings, although flames did actually invade the stage. At the end, there was a parade of victorious revolutionaries, with a large display of flags. . . . The play ended amidst the crowd's applause and cries of "Hao! Hao! Good, good!. . .[and] Long live the Chinese Republic!" which Chinese spectators invariably utter whenever they can no longer contain their pleasure."

A REVOLUTIONARY LEADER EMERGES

The man who had the most to gain from the Wuchang revolt was Sun Yat-sen (1866–1925). Sun was born in Guangdong, near Guangzhou. He was educated in Hawaii and Hong Kong. He studied at

Christian schools and became a doctor. His studies had convinced him that China needed to modernize. It had fallen behind the Western world in science, agriculture, and trade.

Well into the 1900s, life in the Chinese countryside had changed little since ancient times. Peasants made up about 80 percent of China's population. The average peasant farmed a piece of land no larger than 4 acres (1.62 ha), and worked from sunup to sunset just to grow enough food to survive. Few had farm animals; those who did had no more than a pig or two and a few chickens. Peasants did the backbreaking labor of plowing, planting, and harvesting by hand. Most of their harvest went to landowners as payment for use of the land and to local officials who imposed taxes. Police or the military often beat peasants to make sure they complied. Soldiers traveling through villages received food and animals upon demand.

Peasant villages consisted of adobe huts with earthen floors. Greased paper covered the windows. There was no electricity, running water, or indoor plumbing. Theodore H. White and Annalee Jacoby, who worked as *Time-Life* correspondents in China from 1939 to 1945, describe a typical peasant village:

> In his house the peasant stores his grain; in it he keeps his animals at night; in it is the ancestral shrine that he venerates [worships]. By day the street is empty of men. . . . At dusk the men return from the fields, and all over China . . . the villages are covered with a blue haze of smoke that curls from each homestead as the evening meal is cooked. At the

. . . setting of the sun, the same spiraling wisps of smoke go up from the houses to the sky. In the larger villages yellow light may gleam for a few hours from the doorways of the more comfortable, who can afford oil for illumination; but in the smaller villages the smoke fades away into the dark, and when night is come, the village sleeps, with no point of light to break its shadows.

CHINESE REBELS PREPARE TO DEFEND THEIR POSITION AGAINST MANCHU GOVERNMENT TROOPS DURING THE WUCHANG REVOLT.

The Manchu

THE MANCHU WERE A cultural and language group different from the Han Chinese. The Han were the dominant cultural group in China. They considered themselves the "true" Chinese. The Manchu took over China in the 1600s and established the Qing dynasty. The Manchu knew the only way to prevent rebellion was to continue many Han Chinese traditions. These included Confucian values that emphasize harmonious relationships and obeying authority. They set up a government with both Han Chinese, usually referred to as simply Chinese, and Manchu officials. The Manchu leaders had the most power.

The Manchu resisted becoming fully absorbed into Chinese culture. They preserved their own language and banned marriages between Chinese and Manchu. Chinese were not allowed to migrate to Manchuria, and Chinese soldiers were separated from those of the Qing dynasty. The Manchu also dictated dress and hair styles. Male Chinese were required to shave the top of their head and grow a queue, or pigtail, that usually hung down the back, in Manchu style.

When the Qing dynasty ended, revolutionaries immediately began to demand reforms in Manchu styles. Edmond Rottach, a French journalist traveling on a train in China after the revolution, saw one example. "Two uniformed [officials] . . . began at the rear of the train and, moving all the way through it, chopped off every single queue—even the best hidden—with their small scissors," Rottach reported. "I saw over twenty queues thus taken off."

Sun believed that China's ruling family had no interest in addressing social problems, foreign domination of business and trade, or the plight of peasants. Revolution seemed to him to be the only solution. Toward that goal, he organized a group called Revive China Society while in Hawaii during the 1890s.

Sun returned to China in 1895 with plans to seize the port city of Guangzhou in southern China. But the plot failed, and fifteen conspirators were caught, arrested, and executed. Only Sun escaped. He traveled around the world, hiding from agents of the Manchu rulers and seeking money and other aid for his cause. At the same time, the imperial government offered a huge reward for the capture of Sun—dead or alive.

One of the places Sun visited during this time was London, England. There, in 1896, he studied Western forms of representative government. On one occasion, he was tricked into going to the Chinese embassy, where he was arrested and held prisoner on orders of the Chinese emperor. When his British friends found out what had happened, they alerted the police. They worried that Sun would be sent back to China and executed. When the police did nothing, his friends went to the *London Globe*, and the newspaper published a story about the kidnapping. The account caught the attention of British prime minister (and foreign minister) Lord Salisbury. Salisbury intervened to release Sun.

Knowing how the Manchu treated political prisoners, Sun feared he would be tortured and killed during his ten days of imprisonment. He wrote later that he thought his ankles might be "crushed in a vise and broken by a hammer, my eyelids cut off, and, finally, [he might be] chopped to small fragments, so that none could claim my mortal remains." Sun's experience under Chinese captivity in London intensified his desire and efforts to overthrow China's Manchu rulers.

After Sun's release, he continued his revolutionary work and wrote numerous articles and pamphlets that carried his message about overthrowing the Manchu. In 1905 he traveled to Tokyo, Japan, where he founded the National Revolutionary Alliance. This group included Chinese students studying in Japan and a variety of others opposed to Manchu rule. They created propaganda materials that they hoped would encourage people to rise up against the imperial government.

Sun also vowed to fight for broader changes in China. He adopted theories that became known as the Three People's Principles: People's Nationalism, People's Democracy, and People's Livelihood. In his view, the nation should be governed by Chinese citizens, not dominated by foreign countries; government leaders should be democratically elected; and wealth and land ownership should be shared equally among the people. The best way to achieve the People's Livelihood, or the third principle, he said, was through socialism. In the Socialist system, private property does not exist. In addition, the government owns and controls the means of production and distribution for all goods.

SUN YAT-SEN PRESIDES OVER THE FIRST CHINESE PARLIAMENT IN 1912.

Sun as President

When Sun finally returned to China, after the 1911 uprising, he was greeted in Nanjing with a twenty-one-gun salute. On January 1, 1912, delegates from fourteen provinces gathered in Nanjing to elect Sun president of a provisional (temporary) government. The parliament, or lawmaking body, of this government began work on a constitution. At the same time, Sun proclaimed the establishment of the Republic of China. The republic was to be a constitutional democracy, a system of government based on a constitution that establishes the structure and powers of government. On January 5, he issued a manifesto—a declaration of principles. It declares in part:

> The substitution of a republic for a monarchy is not the fruit of transient [passing] passion, but the natural outcome of a long-cherished desire for freedom, contentment, and advancement. We Chinese people, peaceful and law-abiding, have not waged war except in self-defence. We have borne our grievance for two hundred and sixty-seven years with patience and forbearance. We have endeavoured by peaceful means to redress [right] our wrongs, secure liberty, and ensure progress; but we failed. Oppressed beyond human endurance, we deemed it our inalienable right, as well as a sacred duty, to appeal to arms to deliver ourselves and our posterity [future] from the yoke to which we have for so long been subjected. For the first time in history an inglorious bondage is transformed into inspiring freedom. The policy of the Manchus has been one of . . . seclusion and unyielding tyranny. Beneath it we have bitterly suffered. Now we submit to the free peoples of the world the reasons justifying the revolution and the inauguration of the present government.

Sun's manifesto continues with one count after another of injustices committed by the Manchu. These include restricting foreign trade; exercising religious intolerance; unfairly taxing the people without their consent; blocking creation of industries; creating an unfair justice system and inflicting cruel punishments on people charged with offenses; and rejecting reasonable demands for better government. With a new form of government, the manifesto promises

to elevate the people to secure peace and to legislate for prosperity. Manchus who abide peacefully in the limits of our jurisdiction [control] will be accorded equality, and given protection.

We will remodel the laws, revise the civil, criminal, commercial, and mining codes, reform the finances, abolish restrictions on trade and commerce, and ensure religious toleration and the cultivation of better relations with foreign peoples and governments than have ever been maintained before. It is our earnest hope that those foreign nationals who have been steadfast in their sympathy will bind more firmly the bonds of friendship between us, and will bear in patience with us the period of trial confronting us and our reconstruction work, and will aid the consummation [completion] of the far-reaching plans, which we are about to undertake, and which they have long vainly been urging upon our people and our country.

With this message of peace and good-will the republic cherishes the hope of being admitted into the family of nations, not merely to share its rights and privileges, but to co-operate in the great and noble task of building up the civilization of the world.

As promised, the provisional government issued many laws to reform the political, social, and economic systems. But few changes

The Opium War of 1840

YEARS BEFORE THE BIRTH of Sun Yat-sen, the Chinese fought an opium war. During the early 1800s, British merchants were involved in an opium trade that brought them great wealth. They exchanged the drug (produced in India and Turkey) for Chinese goods. The Chinese government wanted to ban opium imports because of its harmful effects on many citizens. Many became addicted to the drug. When the British brought millions of dollars worth of opium into Guangzhou (Canton) in 1839, the Chinese destroyed the drugs. The British responded by seizing Guangzhou, sparking a war in 1840. The war ended in defeat for China and forced the Qing dynasty to sign the Treaty of Nanking (Nanjing) in 1842.

The humiliating terms of the treaty required China to give up some of its territory and control over it. The Chinese had to open ports to foreign trade and allow Great Britain to set taxes on imports. The treaty also gave the British in China the right to be governed by their own laws rather than the Chinese legal system. This provision, called the right of extraterritoriality, meant that Chinese authority over foreigners was almost nonexistent.

Throughout the 1800s, other nations—Russia, Japan, Germany, and France—forced China to sign treaties similar to the Treaty of Nanking. The "unequal treaties," as they became known, were the source of great Chinese discontent, rebellions, and eventually the Nationalist revolution.

actually took place. With a republican government established, revolutionaries lost interest in pressing for reforms. They believed their mission had been accomplished and that their work was done.

Sun was deeply disappointed that his followers did not do more. As he put it, "Without revolutionary reconstruction, what's the use of a revolutionary president?" His disappointment was mixed with the knowledge that he did not have enough power to push the changes forward. And so he resigned in February 1912. Many in the provisional government supported Yuan Shikai, the retired commander in chief of the imperial army, as Sun's successor. They believed that Yuan's military background and strong leadership would strengthen the republic. Even Sun thought that would be the case. He had no idea that Yuan would undermine and eventually attempt to destroy the republican government.

"The substitution of a republic for a monarchy is . . . a long-cherished desire for freedom, contentment, and advancement."

Sun Yat-sen, 1912

YUAN SHIKAI

Yuan came to power at the request of the Manchu government. Or more accurately, Yuan came to power at the request of the emperor's representative. The emperor at the time was just a young boy. The Empress Dowager (wife of the emperor) Cixi had appointed the child, Puyi, emperor before her death in 1908. Because of his age, the government was run by a regent or regency, a person or group who governs until the heir to the throne is old enough to take over.

In November 1911, the regent summoned Yuan to Beijing. Yuan was not in any hurry to come. After the death of Cixi, who had been Yuan's supporter, the regent accused Yuan of treachery against the former emperor. The regent had forced Yuan to leave his post. Yuan was not eager to help the man who had banished him. He stalled until the regent offered him the office of premier, or head of the government.

YUAN SHIKAI, WHO GOVERNED CHINA AFTER SUN YAT-SEN, ATTEMPTED TO UNDERMINE AND DESTROY THE CHINESE REPUBLIC.

Nanjing/Nanking

THE LOCATION OF CHINA'S capital has changed often, but Nanjing (also called Nanking) has served as the capital several times during China's history. Aside from being the heart of government, the city is on the Yangtze River and is an important transportation, commercial, and educational center. Its port serves ships that travel the river to and from the East China Sea and are engaged in foreign trade. The city is also home to numerous historic and cultural buildings such as Sun Yat-Sen's Mausoleum, the Ming Tomb, the King Palace of Taiping Heavenly Kingdom, Pagoda for Buddhist Relics, and the Tombs of Southern Tang Emperors. These and other historical structures are popular tourist attractions.

As part of the bargain, the Manchu agreed to give up the throne and allow the republic to go forward.

Yuan agreed to lead China and command its army. Trainloads of soldiers accompanied Yuan on the journey to Beijing. Two trains with troops arrived before a third train carrying Yuan pulled into the station. Soldiers lined the platforms on each side of the track to protect Yuan. As he got off the train, "the soldiers surrounded and escorted him in such close formation that it looked as though he was being carried in the midst of a huge bunch of bayonets," reported a French journalist who was present.

On February 12, 1912, the dynasty renounced (gave up) the throne of the child emperor. Centuries of dynastic rule came to an end. A republican government with Yuan as its leader was approved. This government, an edict declared, would cooperate with Sun's existing provisional government whose capital was in Nanjing. But Yuan had other plans. He demanded that China's capital be established in Beijing where he had a great deal of influence and army personnel who supported him. To prevent civil war, the revolutionaries agreed to Yuan's plan—as long as he maintained support for the republic.

After Sun gave up his presidency, Yuan assumed the position of China's premier. Not long afterward, the United States officially recognized the new republic with Yuan as its president, and other foreign nations soon did the same. Yuan quickly began efforts to weaken the republican form of government, which he did not favor.

Yuan's Dictatorship

Yuan used his leadership of the large Beiyang Army, the dominant military force within China, to gain power. With the army behind him, he was able to convince or coerce military governors (or warlords) in the provinces to back him.

When an election for parliament was held in 1913, a new political party, the Kuomintang (KMT) opposed Yuan. Also known as the Nationalist Party, the KMT was made up of several revolutionary parties, including one under Sun's leadership. The KMT was headed by Song Jiaoren, a young activist who had helped Sun form the National Revolutionary Alliance in Japan in 1905.

Song was an excellent organizer and gained support by promising to curb Yuan's power. He helped the Nationalists win a majority in the legislature, and the lawmakers made Song leader of the parliament.

Song's leadership was cut short by an assassin in March 1913. Although the evidence strongly suggested that Yuan had a part in the killing, no one could prove he was involved. What is known is that a soldier shot to death the KMT leader while he was standing on a railroad platform in Shanghai, a port city and financial and industrial center in eastern China. Although the assassin was caught and jailed, he died under mysterious circumstances before he could be tried in court. Yuan was also tied to the deaths of several pro-revolutionary generals.

YUAN SHIKAI, CENTER, POSES WITH HIS SUPPORTERS AFTER HIS INAUGURATION AS THE FIRST PRESIDENT OF CHINA IN 1912.

In April 1913, without parliament's consent, Yuan negotiated for a loan from the Five-Power Banking Consortium. This group was made up of banks in Great Britain, France, Russia, Germany, and Japan. Yuan borrowed 25 million pounds (about 100 million dollars). He claimed he needed the money for repaying China's debts to foreign countries and for planned government reforms. Instead Yuan used the money for his own purposes, including propaganda campaigns and bribery to get rid of his opponents and to support his Beiyang Army. With the support of the Beiyang Army generals, who controlled the northern provinces, Yuan insisted that he had sole power to make treaties and declare war.

KMT members in parliament opposed Yuan's underhanded and murderous methods to control government. They declared that Yuan had gone well beyond his constitutional powers. They called for his removal from office. Yuan fought back by removing pro-KMT military governors in the provinces.

Across China on Foot

BRITISH JOURNALIST EDWIN DINGLE traveled across China in 1909, two years before the revolution. During his travels, he received warnings that an uprising against the Manchu was "imminent" but that foreigners would be safe if they did not "assist the Manchus; otherwise, they will be destroyed in a general massacre."

Dingle planned to cross China from Shanghai to British Burma, "1,500 miles [2,414 km] by river and 1,600 [2,575 km] miles walking overland." He started his trip in Shanghai, after traveling there with a companion on a French mail steamer that took them up the Huangpu (Whangpoo) River. Dingle published his account *Across China on Foot* in 1911. He described activity at the Shanghai port where the steamer anchored after days on the river:

> Junks whirled past with curious tattered brown sails, resembling dilapidated verandah blinds, merchantmen were there flying the flags of the nations of the world, all churning up the yellow stream as they hurried to catch the flood-tide at the bar. Then came the din of disembarkation [leaving the ships]. Enthusiastic hotel-runners, hard-worked coolies [laborers], rickshaw [human-powered passenger cart] men, professional Chinese beggars, and the inevitable hangers-on of a large eastern city crowded around me to turn an honest or dishonest penny. Some rude, rough-hewn lout, covered with grease and coal-dust, pushed bang against me and hurled me without ceremony from his path. My baggage, meantime, was thrown onto a two-wheeled van, drawn by four of those poor human beasts of burden—how horrible to have been born a Chinese coolie!—and I was whirled away to my hotel.

The city itself was a mass of congestion. In Dingle's words:

> Trams, motors, rickshaws . . . conveyances of all kinds, and the swarming masses of coolie humanity carrying or hauling merchandise amid incessant jabbering, yelling, and vociferating [shouting], made intense bewilderment. . . . Wonderful Shanghai!

A Second Revolution

Sun could not stand by idly and watch Yuan destroy everything Sun had tried to create. He vowed to overthrow Yuan with the support of the pro-KMT governors and their militias in southern China.

Threatened, Yuan set about to destroy the KMT stronghold in the south. In the summer of 1913, he replaced the southern governors with northern military leaders. He also sent northern army units south to support the replacements. This so angered the southern provinces that seven of them seceded and declared war against Yuan. A second revolution had begun.

In July and August 1913, KMT troops fought Yuan's army, which far outnumbered the KMT. By September the northern army had captured Nanjing, the revolutionary capital, leaving bloody streets and ruined shops and homes. Sun and other rebels fled to Japan.

The Second Revolution seemed doomed from the start. The KMT leadership had not come up with a plan for removing Yuan's government. They had no funds to support their revolution, and the landowners in the provinces were concerned about their own interests and welfare. People in the Chinese countryside had little understanding of the political situation involving Yuan. All they wanted was an end to strife.

With his power intact, Yuan dissolved the KMT, did away with parliament, and appointed a council made up of his followers. The council created a new constitution that made Yuan president for life. But that did not satisfy Yuan. He had further plans—to establish himself as emperor.

CHAPTER 2

Chaos after the Revolution

T HE IMMEDIATE AFTERMATH of China's brief revolutionary period saw disunity at all levels of Chinese society.
Yuan Shikai was not the only one angling for power. Government
officials, gangsters, and local militia in the provinces all hoped to
capture a piece of China for themselves. Government corruption
was common. Bribery, intimidation, and murder were the means
to gain power. Foreign interference in China's affairs, especially
Japan's increasing efforts to take over Chinese territory, grew. No
one paid attention to Sun Yat-sen's third principle, the People's
Livelihood, and few efforts were made to establish economic and
social reforms.

In short, chaos and confusion ruled in most parts of the country,
and no central government could bring the nation together to work
toward common goals. Yuan saw his opening in the revolution's
aftermath. He prepared to assume his place as emperor.

Temple of Heaven

THE TEMPLE OF HEAVEN complex in Beijing represents ancient Chinese religious beliefs. The first temple was built in Nanjing between 1406 and 1420. When the capital moved to Beijing, a replica was constructed there. Only an emperor, as the "Son of Heaven," could pray at the temple and ask heaven to provide a bountiful harvest throughout the land. The emperor went to the place of worship twice each year. He was accompanied by thousands of ministers and eunuchs (castrated males) who served in the royal palace. Commoners were forbidden to watch the solemn procession from the Forbidden City, or imperial palace, to the Temple of Heaven.

In modern times, the Temple of Heaven became part of a beautiful park with elaborate gardens and magnificent structures that are open to local residents and tourists. The buildings in the Temple of Heaven are round. The foundations are square, representing heaven (a rounded dome) and Earth (flat) as they were once imagined to be. One structure called the Altar of Heaven is where prayers were offered for a good harvest. It is constructed on a square base with circular tiers of marble. Each tier is made of stones in multiples of three or nine, representing ancient Chinese numerology. (Numerology is the study of numbers in connec-

At dawn on December 23, 1914, Yuan proceeded to Tian Tan, the Temple of Heaven, in Beijing. For centuries emperors had come to the temple to worship. Emperors typically offered gifts such as animals, grain, jade cups, and silk along with their prayers for good spring harvests and summer rain.

Fearing assassination, Yuan arrived at the temple surrounded by soldiers. One observer describes the scene, noting that Yuan "behaved as on a battlefield. Protected by two rows of soldiers, he proceeded rapidly and silently along the broad avenue leading from the Imperial Palace to the entrance of the Temple. . . . His bodyguards galloped in front of him and behind him."

tion with supernatural events.) The top platform, open to the heavens, is considered the most sacred spot.

Another important structure is the Echo Wall that surrounds the Imperial Vault. A person at one end of the wall can whisper and another person at the other end of the wall can hear the sound. In the courtyard are Triple Echo Stones. If you stand on the first stone and speak facing the Imperial Vault, you can hear a single echo. On the second, you can hear a double echo. On the third stone, you can hear three echoes. Numerous Internet sites provide descriptions and photographs of the Temple of Heaven.

THE TEMPLE OF HEAVEN IN BEIJING WAS CONSTRUCTED BETWEEN 1406 AND 1420.

Yuan wore ceremonial robes and quickly performed the traditional religious rituals. An armored car waited nearby, ready to speed away with him if there were any signs that his life might be threatened.

By respecting the ancient rites, Yuan was making a public statement that the throne would soon be his. Indeed, he helped spread false rumors that the Chinese people wanted the position of emperor to be restored. In late 1915, he called on the national assembly to take a vote. The vote would decide whether he should be emperor. He received unanimous support—nearly two thousand votes in favor of his taking the throne. Naturally, Yuan accepted this decision and began planning for his regime. He ordered a "40,000 piece porcelain dining set . . . a large jade seal and two imperial robes," according to historian and China expert Jonathan D. Spence.

Yuan planned to take the throne as emperor on January 1, 1916, but the powerful Beiyang Army generals who had supported his successful bid to become China's president opposed this latest move.

> *"Every general who could retain the loyalty of his troops, one way or another, became a warlord."*
>
> —Edwin P. Hoyt, journalist, 1989

They did not want a monarchy. The Chinese public also opposed a return to monarchy. After the revolution, they expected to have a republican form of government.

Mass protests against Yuan erupted across China. A group of former revolutionaries in Yunnan, a province in southern China, formed a National Protection Army and prepared for a fight. The army dedicated itself to defending the republic and democracy. In December 1915, it presented Yuan with an ultimatum, demanding that he give up his throne or Yunnan would secede from Yuan's government. Yuan ignored the ultimatum, and the province followed through on its threat. By the spring of 1916, several other provinces had declared their independence.

THE WARLORD ERA

Widespread public disapproval forced Yuan in April 1916 to give up the throne and restore the republic. Two months later, in June 1916,

Yuan died of kidney disease. Yuan's death left the nation without a strong leader. Although China was formally a republic, in reality the central government had little authority. The country was run by dozens of generals who acted more like warlords, each commander in charge of his own military unit and territory. As journalist and historian Edwin P. Hoyt puts it: "Every general who could retain the loyalty of his troops, one way or another, became a warlord."

Most warlords were career (lifelong) military officers. Some were also bandits who took power by intimidation and murder. They ruled diverse territories—from small towns and villages to entire provinces—and trained their armies to be personally loyal to them. Though they were paid for their work, many warlord soldiers had no real allegiance to their commanders. Most soldiers had been jobless, so they fought to earn money rather than for an ideal or out of loyalty. It was not unusual for soldiers to simply abandon their armies during a battle rather than risk their lives and their livelihoods.

Some warlords supported a unified China. They viewed Sun and the KMT as the best hope for unification. Others were more interested in their own goals and led extravagant lifestyles.

Warlords supported their armies financially by taxing land, railroads, businesses, opium sales, and consumer goods within their territories. Warlords also demanded that farmers and villagers provide carts and animals for their troops. Sometimes they allowed their soldiers to loot and pillage homes and shops and keep their takings. Yet money was always in short supply. Soldiers often went without pay for months at a time, while the warlords grew rich and retired to live in luxury.

FAST FACT

BY THE MID-1920s, ABOUT A HALF-DOZEN WARLORD GENERALS CONTROLLED MUCH OF CHINA.

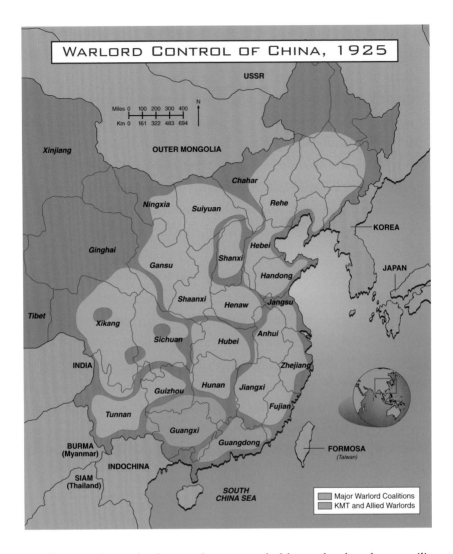

WARLORD CONTROL OF CHINA, 1925

Major Warlord Coalitions	
KMT and Allied Warlords	

Because the warlord generals were not held together by a larger military structure or by allegiance to the nation as a whole, factions (small groups) formed. These factions fought for power, which led to many assassinations. The warlord generals also commonly offered bribes (known as silver bullets) to lure officers from rival factions to their own.

By the mid-1920s, about a half-dozen warlord generals controlled much of China. For example, Zhang Zuolin, called the Old

Marshal, controlled Manchuria and Shandong Province in northern and central China. Feng Yuxiang, who was known as the Christian General (for his Christian faith), ruled the northwest provinces. Wu Peifu, who was considered an expert strategist, became known as Philosopher Marshal. He held Hubei and Hunan provinces along the Yangtze River in central and south central China. The years of warlord rule have been described by historians as a period of confusion and despair in China. But it was not solely the actions of the warlords that created turmoil in China. World War I (1914–1919) and Japanese efforts to control Chinese territory also caused tension.

WORLD WAR I

World War I began in Europe in August 1914. Although China remained neutral for a time, the nation soon felt the effects of the conflict. Its island neighbor Japan had joined the Allies (France, Russia, Britain, Italy, the United States, and others) against the Central Powers which included Germany, Austro-Hungary, Bulgaria, and Turkey. Japan declared war on Germany on August 23, 1914, and quickly seized German settlements and naval bases at the port of Qingdao (Tsingtao) in Shandong Province in northern China. Japan also took over a German-built railroad line and coal mines near this important economic center.

The violation of China's neutrality was one more step in Japan's long-time plan to gain power over the Chinese. Japan and Russia had repeatedly fought over who would control trading and investing rights in Manchuria in China's far northeastern corner. Manchuria was rich with raw materials such as timber, coal, and iron needed for factories. In 1905 Japan had beat out Russia for control of Manchuria. Japan then used Manchuria as a base to further its aggression against the Chinese, believing that it had a "divine mission" to control China.

JAPAN VIOLATED CHINA'S NEUTRALITY IN NOVEMBER 1914 BY LANDING
TROOPS IN QINGDAO (TSINGTAO), CHINA.

In 1915 Japan issued a secret memorandum on China, declaring
that its policy was to make "China voluntarily rely upon Japan. To
force China to such a position there is nothing else for the Imperial
Japanese Government to do but to take advantage of the present
opportunity [war in Europe] to seize the reins of political and financial power."

Japan presented an ultimatum to Chinese officials in January
1915. Japan said it would wage war against China if certain conditions were not met. A document known as the "Twenty-One Demands" listed the conditions. Among the conditions, China had to
agree to Japan's ongoing influence in Manchuria and parts of Mongolia in northern China and absolute control of the seized railroads
and territory in Shandong. The Japanese document also forbade the
Chinese government from ceding or leasing "to a third Power any
harbour or bay or island along the coast of China." In addition, Japan
demanded to participate in China's government and be given police
powers. The Twenty-One Demands required China to consult Japan
whenever the government needed "the service of political, financial,
or military advisers or instructors."

When the Chinese government rejected the agreement, Japan again threatened war. That worried some officials who knew that China did not have the manpower and weapons to win a fight against Japan. Therefore, in May 1915, Chinese officials agreed to most of Japan's demands. However, once the Twenty-One Demands were made public, both the United States and Britain expressed concern. They worried that Japan would cut off China's trade with other countries and would continue its aggression in other parts of Asia. The two countries persuaded Japan to at least drop its demands for control over Chinese policy makers. (After the war, Japan agreed in a 1922 treaty to withdraw all of its twenty-one demands.)

In August 1917, China entered the world war, although it provided no troops. Instead, China sent laborers to aid the European Allies. Because France and Great Britain had suffered severe losses on European battlefields—hundreds of thousands had died—they needed manpower behind the lines. Thousands of poor Chinese volunteered for this labor force, and each person received an immediate payment as well as a monthly sum for his family. Laborers also received clothing, food, and medical examinations.

In Europe, particularly in France, Chinese laborers dug trenches, repaired railroad lines and bridges, constructed barracks, and provided other nonmilitary help. "They worked ten hour days, seven days a week, with some time off allowed for traditional Chinese festivals," reported historian Spence. The workforce allowed Allied troops to stay on the front lines in the fight against the Germans.

BETRAYED

Chinese leaders believed their contributions to the Allied cause would result in Allied demands for a Japanese withdrawal from their country

A Woman's "Place" in China

BEFORE THE NATIONALIST REVOLUTION, Chinese women were at the bottom of a society controlled by a social and political philosophy established by Confucius (551–479 B.C.). A philosopher and teacher, Confucius stressed important virtues such as devotion to parents and family, respect for authority, and harmonious relations.

Traditional Confucian ideology holds that males are superior to females. Women are completely subordinate to men. A girl is required to obey her father and elder brother, and a wife must obey her husband. After a husband's death, a wife is obligated to obey her son. A woman has no right to marry a person of her choice, no right to divorce or obtain custody of her children, no right to education, and no political power.

One of the most harmful forms of oppression of women in China was the custom of foot binding. This practice began with imperialists and the upper class and was copied by peasants well into the twentieth century. The painful practice was supposed to create "golden lilies"—tiny feet considered attractive to men. Usually the binding began when a girl was about five or six years old and continued into her teenage years. Bandages wrapped around her feet kept all but the big toes bent under toward the ball of the foot. The strips of cloth were left on constantly and pulled tighter each night, eventually deforming the foot so that the big toe and heel met, the arch of the foot broke upward, and a girl had to walk— or hobble—on her heels.

and its political affairs. This did not happen. During the peace conference at the end of the war, held in June 1919 at the Palace of Versailles near Paris, France, Chinese leaders learned that Great Britain, France, and Italy had secretly agreed to allow Japan to claim the German territory in Shandong. U.S. president Woodrow Wilson previously had expressed strong support for China on the Shandong issue, but he, too, declared that under international law, Japan had a right to its claim. Paul

A GROUP OF WEALTHY CHINESE WOMEN POSE IN 1910 WITH THEIR BOUND FEET.

Historian John King Fairbank, who lived in China during the 1930s, observed that "all women of middle age or older had bound feet, stumping about awkwardly on their heels as though the front sections of their feet had been amputated. Traveling in the countryside of five North China provinces, we never met a farmer's wife over the age of 30 whose feet were not bound."

With the 1911 revolution (and later Communist and Nationalist uprisings), some efforts were made to stop practices that kept women in subservient positions. Women's groups campaigned for marriage and property rights and opportunities for education. But the basic patriarchal (male-dominated) system did not change much. In rural areas, reforms seldom occurred until after the Communists came to power in the 1940s.

S. Reinsch, an American minister in China from 1913 to 1919, expressed his dismay and embarrassment regarding the U.S. position. He wrote:

> Probably nowhere else in the world had expectations of America's leadership at Paris been raised so high as in China. . . . It sickened and disheartened me to think how the Chinese people would receive this blow which meant the blasting of their hopes and the destruction of their confidence in the equity of nations.

. . . I feared a revulsion of feeling against America; not because we were more to blame than others for the unjust decision, but because the Chinese had entertained a deeper belief in our power, influence, and loyalty to principle.

When Chinese students learned about the decisions made at the Paris peace conference, their anger erupted. Protests spread from university students to merchants and workers across the nation. It was the first time in modern Chinese history that the masses had risen up in an outburst of national protests across the country.

THE MAY FOURTH MOVEMENT

One of the largest protests occurred on May 4, 1919, when students at Beijing National University held a "National Shame Day," marking the anniversary of Japan's Twenty-one Demands. During this demonstration, students protested the rights granted foreigners doing business in their country. They also protested against the war-

Tiananmen Square

TIANANMEN SQUARE IS THE largest public square in the world, covering 100 acres (44 ha). It is named for the huge Tiananmen, meaning Gate of Heavenly Peace, at the northern end of the square. During the time of China's dynasties, however, Tiananmen Square was much smaller and marked the entrance to the imperial city, where emperors and government officials lived and worked. No commoners were allowed to enter the square. After the revolution of 1911, Tiananmen Square became a public place and frequently a site for demonstrations. The 1919 demonstration there set the stage for China's Nationalist movement.

STUDENTS AT BEIJING NATIONAL UNIVERSITY PROTEST ON NATIONAL SHAME DAY IN 1919. THE EVENT MARKED THE CHINESE GOVERNMENT'S CAPITULATION TO JAPAN'S TWENTY-ONE DEMANDS IN 1915.

lord generals who had helped them. Students shouted slogans such as "Cancel Twenty-one Demands" and "Down with Japan." They also demanded that Japan return control of the Port of Qingdao to China. One student deliberately cut his finger to write "Return Our Tsingtao" in blood on a wall.

On that same day, about three thousand students assembled in Beijing's Tiananmen Square. They marched through the capital, handing out pamphlets that explained how the Treaty of Versailles had prevented China from regaining its territorial rights to Shandong. They carried posters with protest slogans and planned to go to the offices of foreign diplomats. But police stopped them, which led to a riot. Marchers went to the home of the communications minister, who was pro-Japanese, and set his house on fire. Squabbles with police broke out, and one student was seriously injured and died in a hospital three days later. It was the only death in this upheaval. Police arrested thirty-two students in the riot. Public pressure over a period of several days brought about their release.

During the month of May, students in other cities shut down schools and boycotted Japanese products. Sun and the Guangzhou government in southern China supported the students. Newspapers around the country did, too. Business people, industrialists, and factory and mill workers joined the protests. So did employees of public utilities, many of whom took part in strikes or work stoppages.

In other protests during May, about two hundred students were arrested and jailed in the Law Building of Beijing University. American professor John Dewey, who was lecturing in China at the time, reported that the "University has been turned into a prison with military tents all around it and a notice on the outside that this is a prison for students who disturb the peace by making speeches. As this is all illegal, it amounts to a military seizure of the University and therefore all the faculty will have to resign." Dewey added that "two students were making speeches and were arrested and taken before the officers of the gendarmes [armed police force]. Instead of shutting up as they were expected to do, the boys asked questions of these officers . . . the officers had them flogged [whipped] on the back." Public pressure forced the police to free the students. Additionally, the government apologized for the students' imprisonment. Clearly, something new was taking root in China in the aftermath of the revolution.

CHAPTER 3

The Struggle to Unify China

SUN YAT-SEN HAD RETURNED to China from Japan in 1916. For three years, he quietly worked on strategies for unifying the country and carrying out the unmet goals of the revolution. In late 1919, he set up a base in Guangzhou to reorganize the KMT and to establish a republican government in that province. By 1921 Sun had become president of the new government, rejecting the rule of the warlord generals who controlled much of the country from Beijing.

In his role as president, Sun sought advice from Western nations on how to solve China's domestic and foreign affairs problems and unite the country. Western governments refused to help. Some officials thought Sun was merely a dreamer. Some thought he did not have the power or backing to bring about change in China. So Sun turned to the Union of Soviet Socialist Republics (USSR). The Soviets offered training and advisers.

Sun did not intend to give up his Three Principles and establish Soviet-style communism in China. (Communism is a system in which a single political party controls the state-owned means of production, with all goods owned in common and available to all as needed.) But he needed help, and when the Soviets offered help, he took it. Thus in early 1923, Sun sent his military aide, Chiang Kai-shek, to Moscow to study the Soviet military and political systems. After three months,

> *"The republic cherishes the hope of being admitted into the family of nations, not merely to share its rights and privileges, but to co-operate in the great and noble task of building up the civilization of the world."*
>
> —Sun Yat-sen, January 5, 1912

Chiang returned to China, and in 1924 Sun founded the Huangpu (Whampoa) Military Academy in Guangzhou. Sun envisioned the academy as training a new generation of military officers who would serve in the new National Revolutionary Army and defend the Nationalist government. He appointed Chiang generalissimo, or commander in chief of the army.

Sun's government also received advice from the Soviets. One adviser, Michael Borodin, was a member of Comintern, a Soviet-sponsored agency whose aim was to establish communism worldwide. Borodin urged KMT leaders to join with the Chinese Communist Party (CCP). His goal was to establish communism in China. Though this was not Sun's goal, the logic of joining the two groups made sense to him.

SUN YAT-SEN, RIGHT, SENT HIS MILITARY AIDE, CHIANG KAI-SHEK, LEFT, TO MOSCOW IN 1923 TO STUDY SOVIET MILITARY AND POLITICAL SYSTEMS.

Whampoa Military Academy

THE HUANGPU (WHAMPOA) MILITARY Academy, China's first modern military training institute, opened in 1924. It was located on Whampoa Island, ten miles (16 km) from Guangzhou. Here, after successfully completing an examination, students studied to be military officers. Between 1924 and 1949, when the "New China" formed, the academy graduated more than thirty thousand officers.

Both the KMT and CCP were represented at the academy. Nationalist Chiang Kai-shek was its first president and Communist Zhou Enlai was head of the political department. But most cadets were anti-Communist and became devoted to Chiang, assisting in Chiang's later efforts to rid the nation of Communists and Red Army troops.

The CCP was small. It had only about fifteen hundred members compared to the KMT's membership of about fifty thousand. But the two groups would have more impact working together than separately to unify the country, so Sun agreed to the plan. The alliance between the KMT and CCP became known as the First United Front.

RAGE AND FRUSTRATION

Sun died of cancer in March 1925, shortly after the creation of the First United Front. Chiang quickly stepped in to take Sun's place. In his role as leader of the First United Front and as commander in chief of the National Revolutionary Army, Chiang began the Northern Expedition. He gathered one hundred thousand troops in Guangzhou and sent them to northern China. The goal was to overthrow three powerful warlord generals—Zhang Zhuolin, Wu Peifu, and Feng Yuxiang.

Chiang's troops consisted of eight armies, or divisions, each sent to a different area. The force included graduates of the Huangpu Military Academy and cadets from other military schools. It also included troops from several provinces as well as some warlord generals who gave up their territorial control to serve in the national military.

The troops were accompanied by CCP activists who met with peasants along the way. They encouraged the peasants to rise up against rich landowners and against the warlord generals who supported them or who were themselves wealthy landowners. The activists stirred the frustrations of peasants who had labored for years under terrible conditions and with little reward. Bolstered by the presence of the army, peasant mobs attacked the landowners. The mobs paraded them through the streets with cone-shaped dunce hats on their heads, a form of humiliation in China. Many landowners were shot to death or beheaded.

As rage and frustration spread through the countryside, workers in the cities also began to show their anger. Chinese workers at Japanese-run textile mills in the port cities of Shanghai, Qingdao, and Tianjin

CHINESE TEXTILE WORKERS STRIKE TO PROTEST THE SHOOTING OF DEMONSTRATORS IN MAY 1925.

engaged in a general strike for higher wages in 1925. In Shanghai, striking workers were locked out of the mill where they were employed. Enraged, they forced their way into the factory, destroying machinery. Armed Japanese guards fired on the strikers, killing one of them.

The shooting prompted demonstrations throughout Shanghai. During one demonstration, six student protestors were arrested and jailed. On May 30, 1925, thousands of Chinese people surrounded the police station where the protestors were held and demanded their release. The officer in charge panicked and called for police backup to break up the demonstration. The police fired on the crowd, killing eleven and wounding twenty.

Word of the attack quickly spread, and over the next few months, demonstrations erupted in other Chinese cities. Though the demonstrations lasted for weeks, they became known as the May 30th Movement. Many of these demonstrations turned violent. During one July rally in Guangzhou, for example, British police shot at protestors, killing fifty-two Chinese and wounding many others. Outraged workers staged major strikes in the British colony of Hong Kong and organized boycotts of British goods. The strikes and boycotts in Hong Kong continued for sixteen months, seriously hurting the island's economy.

Labor unions, backed by CCP activists, encouraged workers to continue their strikes. In March 1927, about six hundred thousand Communist-led workers in Shanghai staged a general strike. They were led by Zhou Enlai, one of the founders of the CCP. Strikers shut down services, factories, mills, ports, and transportation systems throughout the city. They formed a militia of twenty-seven hundred workers and seized police stations, weapons, and city hall.

Strike leaders ordered the protestors not to attack foreign settlements. Although strikers generally obeyed this order, foreigners living or working in these areas feared they would become targets.

IN MARCH 1927, ZHOU ENLAI, ABOVE, LED 600,000 COMMUNIST
WORKERS IN SHANGHAI IN A GENERAL STRIKE AGAINST CHIANG'S
GOVERNMENT.

Organizing the Hong Kong Strike

BRITISH ECONOMIST NIGEL HARRIS explains in his book *Mandate of Heaven* how the Hong Kong strike and boycott of 1925 were organized:

> The strike was directed by a committee of thirteen, responsible to a delegate conference of 800 (in a ratio of one delegate to fifty strikers), meeting twice a week. The committee supervised the feeding, housing and entertainment of the strikers. It requisitioned [converted] gambling and opium dens in Canton as dormitories, rest rooms and education centres. It published a weekly newspaper. Strikers . . . set up a Workers' College with eight . . . schools for adult workers and eight primary schools for their children. These activities were financed by donations, fines and the sale of seized merchandise. To police the boycott, the committee maintained a force of several thousand uniformed and armed pickets [guards] and set up courts to deal with those breaking the regulations. It also maintained a fleet of twelve gunboats to apprehend [catch] river smugglers. Furthermore, strikers spread to the villages to raise support for the boycott and advance the movement for agrarian [farming] reform.

About forty thousand troops from Britain, Japan, Italy, France, the United States, and other countries were brought in to protect the foreigners. A Scottish unit in kilts and playing bagpipes led the way. As the troops marched down Nanjing Road with other troops, one observer noted:

> The U.S. Fourth Marines were a somewhat informal and easygoing troop. Some of them were chewing gum . . . whistling at street urchins, calling out O.K.s and generally earning for themselves the liking of young Shanghai.

The Japanese bluejackets [soldiers], in white leggings with bayonets fixed to the rifles slung across their shoulders, looked fierce and very businesslike.

When Chiang arrived in Shanghai, he congratulated the labor unions for showing restraint during the strikes. The CCP had actively encouraged and organized the strikes. Under orders from Moscow, it tried to keep union members under control. Moscow did not want violence to harm the alliance between the KMT and the CCP. Although it appeared that the two groups were working together, that was not the case.

Chiang had set the stage for an assault against the CCP. On his arrival in Shanghai, Chiang met with bankers, wealthy businessmen, and others, including foreigners, who opposed the Communists. He also met with mobsters known as the Green Gang, a group that controlled an armed force of hundreds.

> *"I am not opposed to the communists, I appreciate their support and sympathy, but I advise them not to take advantage of their influence in the Party to oppress the moderate elements of the Kuomintang."*
>
> —Chiang Kai-shek, March 10, 1927

Then, early on the morning of April 12, 1927, armed gangsters attacked union headquarters and the workers' militia. They were aided by KMT troops loyal to Chiang and police from the international section. In the clash, hundreds of Communists and their supporters were slaughtered. During the following months, Communists and anti-Chiang groups in Guangzhou and other cities were killed or purged (kicked out) from the KMT.

SPLIT IN THE UNITED FRONT

The alliance between the KMT and the CCP was near collapse. Despite the split in the KMT and the growing divide in the United Front, both sides tried to keep up the appearance of unity. The false front held up for only a brief time.

Chiang had always suspected the motivations of the Communists. He believed they were more interested in furthering Comintern goals than in uniting China. In a speech given March 10, 1927, against the left-wing faction of the KMT, he declared:

> The communists have now reached the zenith [height] of their power and arrogance; if their activities are not checked, they will bring disaster upon the Kuomintang. . . . I am not opposed to the communists, I appreciate their support and sympathy, but I advise them not to take advantage of their influence in the Party to oppress the moderate elements of the Kuomintang. If a break were to come about, the revolution would inevitably be weakened.

The Communists did not trust Chiang either. They believed he was secretly planning a permanent breakup between the right and left wings of the KMT. And the Shanghai attack further confirmed their suspicions. On April 27, Zhou wrote to his comrades, urging "Prompt Punitive Action Against Chiang Kai-Shek"—the title of his message. In Zhou's words:

> There have been almost 400 casualties in the recent mass killings and individual arrests and executions of Communists. . . . Chiang has closed Kuomintang party headquarters and

trade union offices, dissolved a municipal government, forced workers to surrender their arms . . . [borrowed] ten million yuan [Chinese money], organized a gang of assassins consisting of hired thugs. . . . He is oppressing the workers, wooing the bourgeoisie, consolidating his political power and getting control of sources of revenue in order to be able to undermine the allegiance of impoverished left-leaning troops.

Zhou warned his comrades not to relax or compromise. "If we again fail to go forward, our power will be shaken in proportion as the enemy advances and we retreat, and political leadership will fall entirely into the hands of the right wing. That will not only dishearten the left wing, it will also inevitably lead to the total failure of the revolution," he wrote.

CHIANG'S ARMY ADVANCES

The years 1926 and 1927 were a confusing time in China. One historian calls these years "one of the most obscure and complicated periods in the history of the Chinese revolution." Internal strife in the KMT, peasant uprisings, labor strikes, and changes in government were a large part of the confusion. But the contest between the Nationalists and the Communists added a layer of complexity to all of these events.

For a time, it seemed that Chiang and his KMT loyalists would in fact be the winners in the battle for China. By the end of 1926, Chiang's Nationalist Army had gained control of seven provinces with a total population of about

> ## FAST FACT
>
> BY THE END OF 1926, CHIANG'S NATIONALIST ARMY HAD GAINED CONTROL OF SEVEN PROVINCES WITH A TOTAL POPULATION OF ABOUT 170 MILLION.

170 million. In the spring of 1927, a division of the army took Nanjing. Chiang set up a right-wing military and civilian government in Nanjing, where he was head of the government and commander in chief of all Nationalist forces.

In July 1927, the Nationalists fought warlord forces in a battle at Xuzhou, an important rail center in central China that Chiang wanted to control. The Nationalists were defeated at Xuzhou and suffered heavy losses. Chiang vowed he would recapture Xuzhou or step down. When he failed to achieve his pledge, he retired. He claimed that he was retiring to promote unity. Some historians think he had other reasons for retiring. He immediately left China for Japan. There, he made arrangements to marry into a very influential family. Chiang married Soong Meiling in December 1927. One of Soong's sisters was the widow of the Nationalist Party's founder, Sun Yat-sen. Another sister was married to H. H. Kong, a wealthy Chinese banker and supporter of both Sun and Chiang. Though Chiang was officially retired from public life, his marriage brought him new, important contacts that would smooth his later return to public office.

CHIANG RETURNS

With Chiang gone, the KMT and CCP joined forces once again. Leaders of both groups planned to again take up the Northern Expedition to defeat the forces of the powerful warlord Zhang. But the alliance could not raise enough money to pay troops to take part in the expedition. As a result, in early 1928, the alliance called on Chiang to return as generalissimo of the Nationalist Army. With the help of wealthy friends and bankers (among them H. H. Kong), Chiang was able to borrow the funds to pay the troops. In April 1928, he led his troops on a march north once more.

CHIANG KAI-SHEK RETURNED TO CHINA IN 1928 TO LEAD THE NATIONALIST ARMY.

Chiang and the KMT won control of warlord-dominated Beijing in mid-1928. That gave Chiang and the Nationalists control of most of China. By the fall of 1928, the Nanjing government became the legitimate government of China and was recognized internationally.

The decade that followed brought badly needed stability to China. China had not experienced a stable government since the revolution had ended the country's long history of dynastic rule.

The years between 1928 and 1937 frequently have been called the Nationalist or Nanjing decade. During these years, Chiang was popular and widely supported. People were thankful that the country seemed unified. The Nationalists began modernizing the legal and penal systems, they banned opium traffic, and increased industrial and agricultural production. Transportation also improved, with highway construction taking place between cities and in rural areas. A new airline, the Chinese National Airways Corporation, was established. Conservation and irrigation projects got under way as well.

Education also improved somewhat, as primary and secondary enrollment increased. Universities also grew and added research programs. Cultural advances during the 1930s included archaeological work and the establishment of a chemical society and mathematical society.

Yet local warlords still threatened the KMT-controlled government. So did CCP leaders in various Chinese provinces. In fact, there were conflicts on many fronts. The stability of the Nationalist Decade was about to end.

CHAPTER 4

Civil War

ALTHOUGH CHIANG KAI-SHEK controlled China between 1928 and 1937, his KMT (or Nationalist) party was badly divided. Much of the right-wing faction supported him, while those on the left wing who had supported the Communists feared him. They had not forgotten the KMT's deadly attacks on the Chinese Communist Party in Guangzhou, Shanghai, and Beijing. Despite its losses, the CCP continued its fight for dominance in China. By the end of 1928, open warfare raged between the Communists and Nationalists. Civil war in China had begun.

A CALL FOR CHANGE

For several years after the 1911 revolution, the CCP had followed the lead of its Soviet advisers. These advisers had urged members to focus their efforts on organizing rebellions among workers in the cities. The

Soviets believed that societal change would begin with working-class citizens. But not all Chinese party members agreed with this strategy. Mao Zedong, for example, favored a different strategy. Mao had established a Communist organization in Hunan Province in 1921. Ten years later, he was elected to the CCP's Central Executive Committee.

MAO ZEDONG ESTABLISHED THE FIRST COMMUNIST ORGANIZATION IN HUNAN PROVINCE IN THE 1920S.

From this influential position, he tried to persuade other party leaders that change in China would require the involvement of the country's massive peasant population, not just its working-class citizens. Mao argued that peasants should be organized into soviets (Communist councils that would govern a local community). He insisted that land should be taken from wealthy owners, who were small in number, and given to the peasants, who were many in number. In his view, the CCP should encourage peasants to join the Communists and become activists. As head of the Peasant Movement Training Institute, which trained peasant leaders to become revolutionaries, Mao sought to involve peasants in the ongoing fight for control of China.

As part of his duties with this organization, Mao spent a month in Hunan to get a first-hand look at how the peasants were organizing there. In a lengthy 1927 report, he noted,

> With the fall of the authority of the landlords, the peasant association becomes the sole organ of authority, and what people call "All power to the peasant association" has come to pass. Even such a trifle as a quarrel between man and his wife has to be settled at the peasant association. . . . The local bullies and bad gentry [upper class] and lawless landlords have been totally deprived of the right to have their say.

Mao's report did not convince the CCP to bring the peasant groups to their cause. But Mao took action anyway. He recruited a small army of about one thousand men. It included Nationalist Army deserters, unemployed miners, armed peasants, and mercenaries (people who fight only because they are paid). In September 1927, he organized a peasant rebellion, with his soldiers lending key support. The rebels attacked small towns in Hunan and Jiangxi provinces during the fall harvest period. Called the Autumn Harvest

Uprising, it was soon defeated by KMT forces. Mao and his army were forced to flee to the Jinggang (Chingkang) Mountains on the border between Hunan and Jiangxi provinces. There Mao made contact with two bandit leaders who agreed to join his forces.

Mao liked this mountainous, lightly populated area. Only about two thousand people lived in small villages in the region. There were no roads, and people traveled by foot or on horses or mules along narrow mountain paths. It was bandit country, and authorities had little or no control over the area. For these reasons, it was a relatively safe place to set up a Communist stronghold. Mao worked with Zhu De (1886–1976), a former warlord who, with his troops, had been purged from the KMT. The two leaders organized peasants, bandits, and rebellious KMT soldiers into troops known as the Red Army. They prepared to fight in a civil war against the KMT's White Army, named for those who had fought against the Communist Red Army

"The Red Army has abolished the mercenary system, making the soldiers feel that they are not fighting for somebody else but for themselves and for the people."

—Mao Zedong, 1928

during the Russian Civil War (1918–1921). Many revolutionaries like Mao and Zhu looked to Russia as a model for China. They differed on whether the peasantry or proletariat should lead the revolution, however. Russia's revolution was about destroying the oppressive regimes of the czars, or emperors.

A Daring Escape

DURING THE TIME THAT Mao was organizing an army, he was captured by KMT troops who were searching for and killing Reds. The soldiers had orders to deliver Mao to headquarters, where he would be executed. He was able to escape and hide in tall grasses as the soldiers pursued him. Mao described his plight in an autobiographical account recorded later by British author Edgar Snow in 1936.

> Many times [the soldiers] came very near, once or twice so close that I could almost have touched them, but somehow I escaped discovery, although half a dozen times I gave up hope, feeling certain I would be recaptured. At last, when it was dusk, they abandoned the search. At once I set off across the mountains, traveling all night. I had not shoes and my feet were badly bruised. On the road I met a peasant who befriended me, gave me shelter and later guided me to the next district.

TRAINING THE RED ARMY

While at their mountain stronghold, Mao and Zhu taught their troops how to be soldiers. Most of the men had no experience with military discipline or loyalty to a cause. Mao insisted that his soldiers follow three basic principles: obey orders; take nothing from the workers and peasants; and share all captured goods.

In a 1928 report to the CCP, Mao noted that even though many of the soldiers were mercenaries, they changed once they had joined the Red Army. Mao wrote:

> The Red Army has abolished the mercenary system, making the soldiers feel that they are not fighting for somebody else but for themselves and for the people. The Red Army has not . . . instituted a system of regular pay, but issues only rice, an

allowance for oil, salt, firewood and vegetables, and a little pocket money. Land has been allotted to all Red Army officers and men who are natives of the border area, but it is rather hard to allot land to those from distant areas.

Part of the training for the Red Army was in guerrilla tactics—small units that could move quickly and launch surprise attacks. As Mao put it, "When the enemy advances, we retreat! When the enemy halts and encamps, we trouble them! When the enemy seeks to avoid a battle, we attack! When the enemy retreats, we pursue!" Years later, Mao wrote a manual on guerrilla fighting that was used to instruct Red Army troops. The first chapter of the manual, "What Is Guerrilla Warfare" begins with an explanation about its necessity:

> In a war of revolutionary character, guerrilla operations are a necessary part. This is particularly true in war waged for the emancipation [freedom] of a people who inhabit a vast nation. China is such a nation, a nation whose techniques are undeveloped and whose communications are poor. . . . Under these circumstances, the development of the type of guerrilla warfare characterized by the quality of mass is both necessary and natural. This warfare must be developed to an unprecedented degree and it must co-ordinate with the operations of our regular armies. If we fail to do this, we will find it difficult to defeat the enemy.
>
> These guerrilla operations must not be considered as an independent form of warfare. They are but one step in the total war, one aspect of the revolutionary struggle. They are the inevitable result of the clash between oppressor and op-pressed when the latter reach the limits of their endurance.

Red Army regiments fanned out across the countryside, aiding Communists who were setting up soviets. In all, about a dozen sovi-

To implement his encirclement strategy against KMT forces, Chiang had 700,000 Nationalist troops, above, compared to 150,000 for the Communists.

ets were established around Jiangxi Province. This is also where Mao moved his base of operations. He had decided that his mountain stronghold was too rugged for quick troop movements, so he set up a base in Ruijin in Jiangxi Province. Ruijin became one of the most important Communist bases in the area.

CHIANG'S ENCIRCLEMENT STRATEGY

As Mao built his army and spread his message of peasant revolution through rural areas of China, Chiang kept a wary eye on his rival. Chiang finally made his move in the early 1930s, with an encirclement campaign against the Communists. When Red Army troops were in the mountains, KMT forces set up checkpoints near the Communist base to prevent Red soldiers from going in or out. In

The New Life Movement and the Blue Shirts

CHIANG KAI-SHEK'S ADMIRATION for German military capability led to his New Life Movement, which he launched in 1934. Its purpose was to militarize the people and to discipline and unify their behavior. Chiang believed that the Chinese should "endure hardship" and be "willing to sacrifice for their nation at all times," as he put it. The movement also encouraged such virtues as honesty and justice as well as politeness and modesty in public.

Supporters of the New Life Movement included a group called the Blue Shirts, named for the rough blue cloth from which their shirts were made. They were headed by Huangpu (Whampoa) Military Academy graduates who had studied under Chiang. These army officers had a fascist leaning. That is, they believed in an elite ruling class and were loyal to Chiang. They wanted him to take the role of a dictator, like Hitler had in Germany. The Blue Shirts strongly opposed communism and were willing to use violence to prove their dedication to Chiang and the Nationalist cause. Their goal was to create a fascist nation.

Neither the New Life Movement nor the Blue Shirts group made a great impact on Chinese life, however. Chiang eventually dissolved both. Some historians believe he did this because they got in the way of his KMT goals.

the civil war battles that followed, both sides lost thousands of men. Chiang declared victory.

In October 1933, Chiang also launched a large-scale campaign against the soviets in Jiangxi Province. Chiang had 700,000 troops compared to the Red Army's 150,000. He also had German help. Earlier, Chiang had turned to Germany and its new Nazi leaders to buy arms. He was impressed with Germany's Nazi dictator Adolf Hitler and his success in militarizing Germany. When Chiang sought German advisers to train his army, Hitler sent German officer Hans von Seeckt to China.

Seeckt advised the KMT to starve out the Communists by preventing food and supplies from reaching them. Backed by planes and heavy guns, the Nationalist strategy was to set up a massive blockade of the Communist base in Jiangxi.

On the other side, Comintern representative Otto Braun advised the Communists to make full-scale frontal attacks against the KMT rather than use guerrilla tactics. The strategy did not work. By early 1934, the Red Army was in danger of total destruction. Braun argued for a retreat from Jiangxi to a Communist base in Hunan, where a division of the Red Army was based.

The Jiangxi Communists discovered that the KMT blockade was weak in the southwest of the province, so the Red Army secretly prepared in the fall of 1934 to move out. Troops packed up rifles, machine guns, ammunition, food, medical supplies, Communist documents and files, printing equipment, and Communist pamphlets. (The pamphlets would be distributed in towns and villages along the way.)

Zhou Enlai, who had fled the KMT when Chiang massacred Communists in Shanghai, had joined leaders of the Red Army. He planned the breakout. About 80,000 (some say as many as 130,000) troops prepared to leave. They were joined by about three dozen women—wives of Red Army officials—and thousands of peasants. Noncombat troops carried the supplies and were guarded by armed soldiers at the rear and sides. About 28,000 troops, many of whom were injured, stayed behind as a rear guard. During the night of October 16, 1934, the Communists slipped out of Jiangxi and began a year-long trek called the Long March. It was an incredible journey of more than 6,000 miles (9,654 km).

> ## FAST FACT
>
> THE YEAR-LONG TREK KNOWN AS THE LONG MARCH EXTENDED FOR MORE THAN 6,000 MILES (9,654 KM).

THE MARCH

By retreating, the Red Army hoped to avoid total destruction. Their goal was to find safety at a Soviet base in northern China.

At the beginning, the troops broke into several columns. They were able to get beyond the KMT defenses in the southwest, marching through Hunan and Guangxi provinces. The forces developed a twenty-four-hour strategy of marching for four hours, then resting for four hours. They were under constant threat from Chiang's army, which pursued them and tried to stop them at mountain passes and river crossings and in towns and villages. KMT bombers flew overhead during daylight hours, attacking marchers. A dozen or more skirmishes or battles took place daily. All the same, the Red Army managed to travel about 24 miles (38.62 km) per day along winding and twisting routes.

Wherever the two armies went, they left behind devastation. Each side wanted to prevent the other from taking or using anything in the villages that would help them advance. A missionary (church worker), who traveled through some of the areas where the two sides fought, reported that he and his companions had trouble finding a place to stay because the villages "had more or less been burned down. The few houses that had been spared were left without doors, windows, frontage [walls], or partitions. All faces [of villagers] expressed sadness and anxiety. When I inquired who the authors of this destruction were I was told, 'on the right bank, it was the Government troops who burned the houses; on the left bank, the Reds.'"

In December 1934, KMT forces attacked the Red Army near the Xiang River in southern China. The Red Army lost about half of its troops, leaving about 40,000 to 45,000 soldiers. But the Communists moved on and were able to take control of several towns in the southwestern province of Guizhou. In January 1935, they captured the Guizhou city of Zunyi. Troops seized supplies of clothes and food and then rested awhile.

While at Zunyi, Communist leaders called a conference of top CCP officials and Soviet advisers, including Braun. At the meeting, Braun's strategy was highly criticized. The criticisms implied that Mao and his mobile guerrilla tactics had been correct after all. More important, the events at Zunyi showed Mao's growing status as a leader in the CCP.

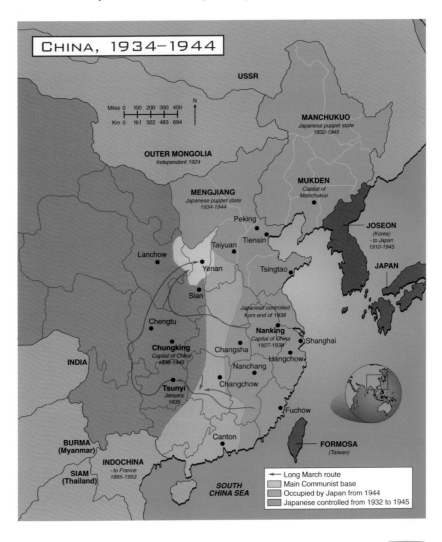

Tales of a Bridge Crossing

FOR DECADES THE CHINESE Communist Party has declared that the Long March (1934-1935) was one of the most heroic events in China's history. No other public view has been allowed. But over the years, researchers have attempted to learn more about the march. A few think that the journey was shorter than originally claimed. In their investigations, they also found different accounts of one of the famous Long March events—the Red Army crossing of the Dadu (Tatu) River.

The river flowed swiftly along a steep gorge. An eighteenth-century chain-link suspension bridge, called the Luding Bridge, was the only way to cross the river. The bridge was paved with wooden planks. Crossing it was "the most critical single incident of the Long March," to use the words of Edgar Snow, a journalist who interviewed Mao in 1936 and wrote about his exploits. Mao told Snow that a regiment of Nationalists had set fire to the planks over the chains on the bridge. The Reds collected doors and coffin lids from peasants to place over the chains while the Nationalists fired their machine guns. According to the tale, twenty-two Red Army men overpowered the Nationalists by throwing grenades at them.

Authors Jung Chang and Jon Halliday, who spent years researching the life of Mao Zedong, declare that the bridge-crossing story "is complete invention. There was no battle at the Dadu Bridge . . . no 'heroic' fighting . . . there were no battle casualties . . . not one was even wounded."

Several other authors reached similar conclusions. For example, in 2004, Chinese-born film producer and author Sun Shuyun retraced the long journey by train and bus. She traveled "through areas little changed to this day." She interviewed forty survivors of the Long March, "ordinary people who were left behind or managed to reach the end." She found that "There was only a skirmish over the Dadu River."

Still there is no doubt that the troops on the Long March endured terrible conditions. Stories about their triumphs over hardship likely will be told for years to come.

From Zunyi, the Red Army resumed its march, moving west and north from one province to another over mountains and through swamps. In some mountainous terrains, they faced treacherous canyons and snow and ice storms. The arms, legs, fingers, and toes of some soldiers froze and had to be amputated. Food was scarce and soldiers went without eating for days. The marchers eventually began a perilous trudge over the Great Snow mountain ranges through a pass 10,000 feet (30,480 m) high. Fog and rain that turned to hail created problems for the men. Most soldiers from southern China were not used to the cold and had only thin clothing to protect themselves. As one soldier noted: "Our breath froze and our hands and lips turned blue. Men and animals fell into chasms and disappeared. Those who sat down to rest or relieve themselves froze to death on the spot."

COMMUNIST TROOPS GATHER AT THE GREAT WALL IN 1938 TO COMMEMORATE THE END OF THE LONG MARCH.

The marchers ran out of food and lived on barley grown in the mountains, often eating it raw. Beyond the mountains, two branches of the army came together. One branch was led by Mao, and another column, which had traveled a different route, was led by Zhang Guotao. The leaders spent days discussing their next move. Mao wanted to go northeastward to Shaanxi (or Shensi) Province to establish a soviet. Zhang's plan was to go west to Xizang, a region near Tibet. Mao and Zhang could not agree, and the branches split again.

Mao's troops traveled across a valley with grasslands and muddy swamps. Many of the men were stricken with dysentery, malaria, body lice, hunger, thirst, and exhaustion. Deserters were numerous. By October 1935, the Red Army, whose troops had lost tens of thousands of men, reached a mountainous and remote area in Shaanxi. Zhang's forces had fared even worse. What was left of his army managed to make it to Yenan (Yan'an) in Shaanxi where the Communists had set up headquarters.

After slogging some 6,200 miles (10,000 km), the march ended with fewer than eight thousand troops. This was about one-tenth of the number that had started the journey. Nevertheless, they were able to set up a Communist base in the far north, transferring power from the southern part of the nation. But the chaos and conflict of the postrevolutionary period was far from over.

CHAPTER 5

War with Japan

Tracted many Chinese from the growing threat posed by Japan. During the 1920s, Japanese military leaders pressed for expansion of Japan's territory.

Japan needed raw materials for its industries and land and jobs for its growing population. Manchuria, in China's far northeastern corner, had an abundance of all three. Although Japan already controlled trade and investment in Manchuria, along with its ports and railroads, Japanese leaders were not satisifed. In 1931 Japan seized Manchuria and made it a Japanese state called Manchukuo. Over the next six years, Japan steadily expanded its influence in northern China, ultimately leading to war between the two countries. The war that began in 1937 pitted the powerful Japanese military against a weak and splintered China.

Uniting against the Japanese

As Japanese aggression increased during the Chinese civil war, the Chinese Communists began calling for an end to the fighting and for China to unite against the Japanese. Many people across China felt this way. They feared that Japan would win control over all of China if the Communists and Nationalists did not unite to fight this threat.

Fast Fact

MANY CHINESE PEOPLE FEARED THAT JAPAN WOULD WIN CONTROL OVER ALL OF CHINA IF THE COMMUNISTS AND THE NATIONALISTS DID NOT UNITE AGAINST THE JAPANESE THREAT.

Chiang Kai-shek did not consider stopping Japanese aggression to be a priority, however. He knew that his armies could not win against the more powerful and better-armed Japanese forces. Moreover, he was determined to destroy the Communists first, unite the country, and then face the Japanese.

In 1936 Chiang began to assemble a force of three hundred thousand men and one hundred aircraft to wipe out the Red Army. He met with Generals Zhang Xueliang and Yang Hucheng to plan for the campaign. Zhang, a warlord and former ruler of Manchuria, had a large army that had remained with him when the Japanese forced him out of Manchuria.

On Chiang's orders, Zhang's army had been fighting Communist forces in Xi'an, the capital of Shaanxi Province in central China. But Zhang had become increasingly frustrated with Chiang. Zhang and his troops believed it was foolish to concentrate all of their resources on eliminating the Communists rather than stopping the Japanese invaders. In fact, many members of Zhang's army had organized the Society of Comrades for Resistance against Japan.

CHIANG KAI-SHEK, RIGHT, WITH ZHANG XUELIANG, LEFT, IN 1930.
ZHANG WOULD LATER BE INVOLVED IN CHIANG'S KIDNAPPING.

Zhang himself had met with the CCP's Zhou Enlai in an attempt to plan an end to the civil war.

KIDNAPPING CHIANG

Zhang and Yang tried to explain to the Nationalist leader that students and others were protesting the civil war and calling for a united front against Japan. Such news did not impress Chiang. He was stubborn (some historians say he was arrogant) and believed his way was the right and only way. The generals tried to reason with Chiang, but he angrily refused to change course and threatened to kill the protestors.

> *"When the students of Xi'an demonstrated for national salvation, police were ordered to open fire at these patriotic youths. Anyone with a conscience could not have let things go so far!"*
>
> —General Zhang Xueliang and
> General Yang Hucheng, 1936

The two generals decided to take matters into their own hands. On December 12, 1936, Zhang's soldiers attacked the villa where Chiang was staying and killed his bodyguards. The commander in chief fled the villa in his nightshirt, jumped over a backyard wall, injured himself, and hid in a mountainside cave. Zhang's soldiers quickly captured and arrested Chiang.

MADAME CHIANG KAI-SHEK, PICTURED HERE IN 1937, WAS
INSTRUMENTAL IN GAINING THE RELEASE OF HER HUSBAND, LEFT,
FROM HIS KIDNAPPERS.

Zhang and Yang immediately sent a telegram to national and
world leaders. The message scolded the generalissimo for being "mis-
led" and "divorced from the masses of people." It declared in part:

> We—Zhang Xueliang and Yang Hucheng—have repeatedly
> offered [Chiang] our earnest remonstrances [opposing views]
> only to be harshly reproached [criticized]. When the students
> in Xi'an demonstrated for national salvation, police were or-
> dered to open fire at these patriotic youths. Anyone with a
> conscience could not have let things go so far! Having for

long years been colleagues of the Generalissimo, we could hardly sit by idly. So we offered him our last remonstrance for the sake of his personal safety and in order to stimulate his awakening.

Chiang was held captive for two weeks. During that time, Zhang and Yang and other military leaders discussed their options. Some thought Chiang should be killed, but others worried that Chiang's death would bring even more disorder in China. The public began to call for Chiang's release, arguing that Chiang was needed to help bring about unity. One of the strongest supporters of engaging Chiang's help in bringing the country together was the Russian dictator, Joseph Stalin. Stalin knew that a unified China would be a much more forceful opponent to Japan, which was also Russia's enemy, than a divided China. Stalin argued for a united front and insisted that Zhang was not powerful enough to bring that about. In Stalin's view, Chiang was the only one who could do it.

Many talks and much negotiating took place. Among those actively seeking Chiang's release was Chiang's wife, Madame Chiang Kai-shek. Madame Chiang was a strong supporter of the Nationalist cause. Her efforts helped win her husband's release in December 1936. She wrote a letter to Zhang while Chiang was in captivity. She asked Zhang to consider the welfare of the nation in dealing with her husband. She also wrote to the generalissimo, criticizing him for his temper. "You never patiently explain things to your subordinates. Also you never listen to their opinions," she wrote. She added, "The officers and men of the Northeastern Army have been driven out of their homeland by the Japanese and it is only natural that they demand resistance to Japan. You should have told them what is in your mind and never hurt their anti-Japanese feelings."

Chiang's captors agreed to his release in exchange for Chiang's agreement to a proposal for unification. It included pledges to:

- Reorganize the Nationalist government to consist of not only Nationalists but also Communists and other anti-Japanese members.

- Release political leaders whom Chiang had imprisoned in Shanghai.

- Bring together the Red Army and the Nationalists to resist Japan.

- Set up a national conference to establish a policy against Japanese aggression.

- Withdraw Nationalist Army units from Shaanxi and allow the armies of Zhang and Yang to control the province.

Chiang agreed to the proposal and was released on December 25, 1936. The next day, Zhang accompanied Chiang on a flight to the Nationalist capital in Nanjing. There the generalissimo was warmly greeted by hundreds of thousands of supporters. He regained his position as national leader and took immediate action against Zhang for his betrayal. He had Zhang placed under house arrest [confined to his house] and then took advantage of Zhang's former addiction to opium. He gave Zhang the drug and allowed his one-time loyal general to became addicted again. From that point on, Zhang faded from the revolutionary scene.

A BRIEF ALLIANCE

Chiang used his influence to forge an agreement between the KMT and the CCP in early 1937. The two sides agreed to take part in a Second United Front to resist Japanese aggression. As

**CHIANG, RIGHT, AND MAO, LEFT, TOAST TO THEIR BRIEF ALLIANCE
AGAINST THE JAPANESE IN 1937.**

part of that agreement, the Communists gave up their efforts to
overthrow the Nationalist government. They stopped taking land,
and they gave control of the Red Army (which became known as
the Eighth Route Army) to the Nationalists. In exchange, the Nationalists promised to end attacks on Communist bases, to release
all political prisoners, and to prepare immediately for resistance
against the Japanese.

For a time, Communist and Nationalist forces cooperated toward
their shared goal of eliminating Japan from China. But differences
between the two sides had only faded, not disappeared. The Communists expanded their operations in northern China and increased
the number of troops stationed there. Chiang saw these moves as
a threat to the Nationalists and his role as China's supreme leader.

He believed the Nationalists had to be in control once the Japanese were forced out of China. So, although there was once more a united front, it was not destined to last long.

WAR BEGINS

Tensions between Japan and China increased in late June and early July 1937. Japanese troops were practicing military maneuvers near the Lugou Bridge, also known as the Marco Polo Bridge, just outside Beijing. During the maneuvers, Japanese and Chinese soldiers exchanged fire. When a Japanese soldier did not answer roll call on the morning of July 7, officers demanded that they be allowed to search for him. Chinese troops did not comply. A shooting confrontation began that sparked eight years of war between Japan and China.

A MAN HELPS TWO YOUNG CHILDREN WHO HAVE BEEN INJURED IN A JAPANESE BOMB ATTACK ON THE SHANGHAI RAILROAD STATION IN 1937.

In late July, the Japanese seized control of Beijing. Then in August 1937, they advanced on Shanghai where Chiang decided to resist. But as journalist Theodore H. White put it, "There was no hope of success in matching Chinese flesh against Japanese metal; a withdrawal might have salvaged [saved] some of the good units of the Chinese army for later operations in the hinterland [outer areas], where they could meet the Japanese on more nearly even terms. . . . [But] Chiang's stubbornness refused to submit to them."

From September through November, the Chinese at Shanghai resisted but failed to hold the city. The Chinese army retreated. The Japanese then advanced on the Nationalist capital of Nanjing. In early December, two divisions of Japanese troops, supported by Japanese navy fleets, attacked the city. Over the next six weeks, Japanese forces committed atrocities that have been called among the most brutal in world history. In what is known as the "Rape of Nanking," an estimated 300,000 to 400,000 Chinese were killed—gassed, bayoneted, burned or buried alive, machine-gunned, or mutilated until dead.

FAST FACT

AN ESTIMATED 300,000 TO 400,000 CHINESE PEOPLE WERE KILLED DURING THE JAPANESE ATTACK IN 1937–1938 KNOWN AS THE "RAPE OF NANKING."

Some 20,000 women, young girls, and elderly nuns were raped and then killed. People trying to escape by crossing the Yangtze River were shot. So many died that bodies clogged the river.

An eyewitness account by a *New York Times* reporter, Frank Tillman Durdin, was published on December 18, 1937. He reported widespread deaths of civilians and looting of buildings throughout the city. The report also describes mass executions of Chinese soldiers and those suspected of being in the military. "Nanking's streets

JAPANESE SOLDIERS CAPTURED THE WALLED CITY OF NANKING IN DECEMBER 1937.

were littered with dead. Sometimes bodies had to be moved before automobiles could pass," Durdin wrote.

The Japanese captured the gates to the walled city, and at one gate, they killed a mass of Chinese defenders. They "were piled up among the sandbags, forming a mound six feet high," according to Durdin. The dead remained there for days, and military vehicles crunched "the remains of men, dogs and horses." Apparently the Japanese wanted "the horrors to remain as long as possible, to impress on the Chinese the terrible results of resisting Japan," Durdin wrote.

With the fall of the Nationalist capital, the Japanese believed that Chiang would negotiate a peace settlement. But they were wrong. The capital was moved to Hankou, near Wuhan on the Yangtze River. (Chiang's headquarters were in Chongqing in western China's Sichuan Province.)

Wuhan fell to the Japanese in late 1938. So did other major cities along China's eastern coast. Chinese resistance, no matter how fierce, could not overcome the superior Japanese forces. The Japanese gained control of the entire coastal area as well as major rivers, industries, and railroads. They did not push into the interior regions because they "felt that they could wait until a paralysis of all economic

"The Nanking Safety Zone"

IRIS CHANG'S CAREFULLY RESEARCHED book *The Rape of Nanking* provides detailed descriptions of Japanese atrocities. It also includes a chapter called "The Nanking Safety Zone." It is an account based on many interviews and diaries of a small group of "Americans and Europeans who risked their lives to defy the Japanese invaders and rescue hundreds of thousands of Chinese refugees from almost certain extermination." The group of missionaries, doctors, professors, and business people were able to negotiate with the Japanese to set up a safety zone for nonmilitary citizens. The safety zone was near the center of the city where a university, women's college, and government buildings were located. In spite of incredible odds against them, the group managed to ward off the constant threats of the Japanese, and the Safety Zone "eventually accommodated some 200,000–300,000 refugees."

A Japanese soldier overlooks a devastated Nanking. The Japanese occupation of the city in 1937 was particularly brutal.

and transport functions brought Chinese resistance to a halt," *Time-Life* journalists White and Jacoby reported.

What about the People?

Hundreds of thousands of Chinese citizens were killed in the bloody battles against the Japanese. But millions also moved out of the eastern cities "in one of the greatest mass migrations in human history," according to White. Many made the trek on foot. Unskilled laborers did most of the heavy lifting, carrying goods by balancing bamboo poles on their shoulders. People also traveled by rail or river. On the waterways, row boats, steamers, pontoons, or native junks (sailing vessels) moved the masses and supplies.

The staff and students of universities saved their libraries, laboratories, and engineering schools by carrying their contents and other goods on boats or pack animals to inland areas. Even cattle raised by a university's agricultural department were herded to inland areas.

Workers took apart industrial machinery and carried parts westward across mountains to the interior. There they set up factories. Shop and restaurant owners and other business owners packed up their merchandise and joined the trek. So did peasants who fled the Japanese and the flooding caused by Chinese armies opening dikes (waterways) to stop Japanese troops from advancing.

Estimates of the number of people who moved inland during this time range from 3 million to 25 million. But the majority stayed in eastern cities, towns, and villages. Many decided not to flee because they did not want to lose their jobs or farms. They chose to take their chances with the Japanese.

COLLAPSE OF A UNITED FRONT

Week after week, month after month, the war went on, with the Japanese claiming most of the victories. By about 1939, 1 million Japanese forces held the coast, railroads, and rivers. But the Nationalist and Communist forces did not give up. The Nationalists fought in the southwest while the Communists battled in the northwest. The Nationalist capital, which had been moved to Chongqing on the upper Yangtze some 700 miles (1,126 km) from the coast, suffered regular air raids by Japanese bombers. Chiang's small air force was unable to fight back effectively.

Guerrilla warfare by the Communists was not very effective against the Japanese. However, they were able to ambush Japanese troops, kill guards at city walls by sniper fire, and capture Japanese weapons and other supplies.

As the fighting wore on between Chinese and Japanese forces, China's Nationalists and Communists continued their efforts to gain support, territory, and power. Both sides anticipated the day when Japanese forces would leave their country and one or the other would take control of China. As a result, from 1939 to 1941, Communist and Nationalist troops fought each other as much as they battled the Japanese. To reduce the internal conflicts, each side agreed to a defined area where it would fight the Japanese.

CHINESE NATIONALIST TROOPS ARE SHOWN PERFORMING GUNNERY PRACTICE IN THE 1930S. EVEN AS ALLIES, COMMUNIST AND NATIONALIST TROOPS FOUGHT EACH OTHER AS MUCH AS THE INVADING JAPANESE.

Part of the agreement involved moving troops, formerly under Communist command, that had become part of the National Revolutionary Army under Chiang. Chiang ordered the Communist Eighth Route Army to move north of the Yellow River in coastal Jiangsu (Kiangsu) Province. The Red guerrilla forces in southern provinces that the Nationalist government had reorganized and renamed the New Fourth Army were to locate north of the Yangtze River. What followed next is unclear. Each side told a different story.

According to the Communists, part of the New Fourth Army traveled north, but officials, staff, and about five thousand troops remained at headquarters. They were ready to move out but refused to take a route set by the Nationalist government. The route would lead to Japanese posts on the river. General Zhou Enlai pleaded with Chiang to change the army's course. Chiang approved the change. But some eighty thousand Nationalists surrounded and attacked the New Fourth Army at their headquarters, leaving thousands of casualties.

The Nationalists' version says that the New Fourth Army Incident, as it became known, was caused by Communists who did not honor their agreement and deliberately delayed their trek north. Nationalists declared that the Communists planned to increase their territory and, toward that end, attacked government forces.

Whatever the truth of the matter, the 1941 massacre created a new strain between the Communists and Nationalists. After all the battles, loss of life, and political maneuvering in the aftermath of the revolution, efforts to unite China appeared doomed. The two sides grew even further apart. It seemed unlikely that they would ever be able to work together for a united China.

CHAPTER 6

China in World War II

WHILE CHINA WAS DEALING with internal conflict and Japanese aggression, World War II had begun in Europe with the German invasion of Poland in 1939. One after another, the countries of Europe fell to Adolf Hitler and his Nazi military machine. In 1940 Italy and Japan joined Germany to form an alliance known as the Axis. Fighting against the Axis were the Allies, which at first included Great Britain and the Soviet Union—and in 1941 the United States and China.

The United States had tried to stay out of the war. Americans at the time wanted nothing to do with another war in Europe. World War I had claimed more than 116,000 American lives. Many Americans wanted to sit out this new European war. That changed on December 7, 1941, when Japan bombed Pearl Harbor, a U.S. naval base on the Pacific island of Hawaii. The next day, President Franklin D. Roosevelt declared war on Japan. The United States joined the Allies in their fight against Germany, and the Allies joined the Americans in their fight against Japan.

CHINA JOINS THE FIGHT

Before this time, the United States had paid little attention to China's war with Japan. Now, with the American declaration of war against Japan, that conflict took on new importance. The United States saw the China-Japan conflict as another way to keep the pressure on Japan. And, with China as an ally, the United States could launch attacks from Chinese soil. From 1941 to 1945, the United States' strategy was to keep China actively fighting Japan so that the United States could prepare to attack Japan from China. The more the Japanese were battling the Chinese, the fewer men and materials the Japanese would have to fight other Allied forces.

With China as an ally, the Americans faced an uncomfortable choice. They had to decide which group of Chinese to deal with—the Nationalists or the Communists. The U.S. government sided with Chiang Kai-shek and the Nationalists. This decision resulted from several factors. Chiang already had strong ties to the United States. In addition to that, the KMT (and even Madame Chiang) worked hard to convince American officials that they were worthy of U.S. support. What is more, the KMT's military wing was stronger at this time than the Red Army. These were some of the factors that led to the U.S. decision to provide the KMT with millions of dollars in equipment, supplies, and funds.

FAST FACT

IN THE EARLY 1940s, THE NATIONALIST ARMY HAD AN ESTIMATED 3.8 MILLION TROOPS. BUT MANY WERE POORLY TRAINED OR NOT TRAINED AT ALL.

The United States began sending military and financial aid to China's Nationalist government in late 1941. U.S. officials hoped the aid would help modernize the Chinese army. China badly needed help if it was going to successfully fight Japanese forces in China. The Nationalist Army was said to have 3.8 million troops at that time. However, many were poorly trained or not trained at all. Most troops

U.S. ARMY OFFICERS TRAIN CHINESE OFFICERS IN WARFARE AS PART OF THE MILITARY AND FINANCIAL AID TO THE NATIONALIST GOVERNMENT IN 1941.

were from poor families. Many suffered from ill health even before they reached the war zone. In 1943 alone, 750,000 out of nearly 1.7 million draftees never made it to the front lines because they were too ill to fight or because they died along the way.

THE CHINA-BURMA-INDIA MISSION

In mid-December 1941, Japan entered the British colony of Burma (modern-day Myanmar) on China's southwest border. The Japanese blockaded the Burma Road. This vital route for transporting American war supplies to China passed through mountainous territory. The supplies were shipped to India first and then on to China and Chiang's army via Burma.

When Japanese soldiers cut off the Burma Road, the only way to move troops, aviation gas, oil, and other supplies from India to China was across the rugged Himalaya mountains. This mountain range rises 20,000 feet (60,960 m) and higher. In the 1940s, flying over the Himalaya mountains in twin-engine planes was a challenging experience. The planes faced unpredictable weather and wind currents. Transporting cargo over the mountains "presented a seemingly impossible operational challenge," according to a U.S. Army Air Force report. But "soldiers and airmen, [and] troops in the region reduced the Himalayas by way of semantics [words], simply referring to them as 'The Hump.'"

Pilots flying over the Himalayas were part of an American civilian group. All were volunteers who had flown for the U.S. Army Air Force. They and their ground crew were known as the Flying Tigers. The group's planes were easy to spot because of two images painted on them. On one side of each plane was a pouncing winged tiger. And under the nose, painted shark's teeth made the planes look like hungry sharks heading for their prey.

One of the Flying Tiger group was Colonel Robert Scott who wrote *God Is My Co-Pilot* after the war. He recalls his first encounter flying over Japanese troops traveling on the Burma Road:

> Keeping very low . . . I turned East and found the Burma Road, turned up it and started looking for the column which I knew

The Burma Road

HUNDREDS OF THOUSANDS OF Chinese laborers built the Burma Road after the start of the Chinese war with Japan in 1937. Working by hand, men, women, and children lugged rocks in baskets and hacked at the earth with axes. They used bamboo tubes full of gunpowder to blast apart boulders. Rains, mud, and rugged mountains created hazards to health and life. Many workers died from disease, accidents, and lack of food.

The Burma Road was completed in 1938. It turns and twists in narrow lanes over 700 miles (1,126 km) from a railhead in northeastern Burma to Kunming, China. Allied war supplies that landed by plane or ship in India were shipped by rail to Burma. Trucks then carried goods overland to Kunming. For a time, it was the only way to move Allied war supplies across the mountains. Along the route, convoys often suffered bad weather, flimsy bridges over gorges, landslides, and lack of communication.

THE BURMA ROAD, AERIAL PHOTO AT RIGHT, WAS A VITAL SUPPLY LINE TO ALLIED FORCES OPERATING IN CHINA.

were Japanese. I approached them from the rear, fired from a thousand yards, and the road seemed to pulverize. The closely packed troops appeared to rush back towards me as my speed cut the distance between us. I held the six guns on as I went the length of the troop column and caught the trucks. . . . Straight back to the base I went, feeling very intoxicated with success.

Frank Moraes, a war correspondent from India, was a passenger in a Flying Tiger cargo plane during the 1940s. He recalls that the plane flew

over the Hump from an airfield in the northeast corner of India to Kunming [China]. . . . We had taken off from our Indian airfield two hours after midnight and flew high through grey vapoury clouds in an inky void. . . . The cold

Flying Typers

JOURNALISTS WHO WERE ON Flying Tiger air-cargo flights were called Flying Typers because of the small, portable typewriters they carried. In remembrance of these World War II aviation reporters, a Flying Typers website presents some of their adventures. A 2006 story about flying the "Hump" notes:

Aircraft would encounter up and down drafts, falling and rising thousands of feet in almost an instant.

At another moment without warning, an airplane would be flipped over by wind currents or whipped side to side. . . .

During the three plus years of Hump operations, more than 167,285 trips were completed, delivering 760,000 tons of air cargo.

But the price was paid by 792 lives lost aboard 460 aircraft and in 701 major accidents.

Incredibly . . . in 2006 sixty-four years later, remains of Hump pilots and their downed aircraft are being recovered.

was numbing. It oozed through the thick soles of my United States army boots and through my fur-lined gloves. Sitting inside that huge lumbering plane in huddled heaps wrapped in greatcoats and rugs, with parachutes strapped to our backs and oxygen masks on our faces, we looked like phantoms from a . . . nightmare.

Despite American efforts, the Japanese continued their advance into Burma. In 1942 Roosevelt appointed General Joseph W. Stilwell, a former military attaché to China, to take charge of America's military operations in Burma. These operations were called the China-Burma-India (CBI) mission. General Stilwell was known as "Vinegar Joe" because of his harsh and outspoken manner. He was sent to China to serve as America's representative and as Chiang's chief of staff. He would also supervise handouts of U.S. supplies and equipment.

STILWELL AND CHIANG

At first Chiang accepted this arrangement. But soon the relationship between the two men soured. Some historians say that Chiang and Stilwell hated each other. Chiang viewed Stilwell as arrogant and power driven. Stilwell expressed contempt for Chiang, accusing him of cowardice.

The two men increasingly disagreed on tactics and goals. Stilwell believed his main duty was to train the Chinese ground forces so that they could drive the Japanese out of northern Burma. He believed the Nationalists and Communists should join forces to stop the Japanese. He did not support the Communists, but he viewed their soldiers as better fighters than the Nationalists.

Chiang, on the other hand, argued that increasing his country's air power with the help of the United States was key to getting

GENERAL STILWELL, FAR RIGHT, POSES FOR THE PRESS WITH CHIANG AND HIS WIFE IN 1942.

the Japanese out of China. He insisted that his ground troops—about four hundred thousand in number—belonged elsewhere. They should be used to blockade the Chinese Communist areas in Yenan. Chiang saw Stilwell as interfering in China's political affairs, and he was ready to ask the United States to recall its representative. However, Madame Chiang convinced the generalissimo that such an action would not meet with U.S. approval.

Stilwell continued efforts to open up supply lines to China. He planned to send troops from both the east and the west to attack Japanese troops holding the Burma Road. He urged Chiang to lift the blockade against the Communists and let some Communist soldiers fight alongside the Nationalist troops. Chiang refused. He insisted that he had to keep up the fight against Communist strongholds in the northwest.

Disagreements between Chiang and Stilwell continued as Japanese troops moved farther into Burma. In the spring of 1942, British soldiers were driven back to Yangon (Rangoon), the capital. Stilwell and his troops tried to keep the Burma Road open. But Chiang refused to commit enough Nationalist soldiers to get the job done. Chiang's troops, except for two divisions, returned to China. General Stilwell stayed with the remaining soldiers, refusing to escape on a cargo plane sent to fly him and his staff out. In May 1942, Stilwell led a retreat of about one hundred soldiers and civilians along jungle trails to Ledo in India.

Fred C. Robins, who served with a special service unit in India and Burma during the CBI mission, reported in his diary that "Conditions were ghastly along the trails. Swarms of disease-bearing insects beset the refugees who also suffered from lack of food, impure water, and early monsoon [annual heavy rainfall] conditions. Deaths were counted in many thousands."

After leaving the jungle, Stilwell reorganized his forces and went on for the next year to try to reclaim territory taken by the Japanese. At the same time, he and Chiang argued about tactics. President Roosevelt was worried that the fight against the Japanese might be lost in China. He urged Chiang to allow Stilwell to command all Chinese ground units. Chiang rejected Roosevelt's proposal, and instead again asked that Stilwell be withdrawn. The president became convinced that Chiang would never yield, and he recalled Stilwell on October 19, 1944. General Albert C. Wedemeyer replaced Stilwell.

War in the Pacific

As World War II ground on in Europe, Japan increasingly struck in the Pacific, seizing territory in the Philippines and Southeast Asia. Beginning in mid-1944, the Japanese launched kamikaze attacks. In these attacks, pilots on suicide missions deliberately flew their planes, loaded with explosives, into Allied ships and other targets. The United States had to decide whether to concentrate its forces against Japan or to focus on fighting Germany in Europe. The U.S. government agreed with Great Britain that Germany had to be defeated first, and then more forces would be available to attack Japan.

When Germany finally surrendered on May 7, 1945, the Allied focus turned to the Pacific. Allied marines, soldiers, and sailors liberated island territories under Japanese control. These included Guadalcanal, the Solomon Islands, the Philippines, and Iwo Jima. The Soviets had also seized some northern Japanese islands and taken control of parts of Manchuria.

While battles were going on in the Pacific, Chinese forces stopped many Japanese advances in China. They did so under the command of Wedemeyer, who was able to improve the training of Chiang's Nationalist soldiers. Unlike his predecessor, Wedemeyer did not insist on bringing in Communist forces to fight with the Nationalists.

In spite of some successes, Chinese forces met strong resistance both in Burma and China. They simply could not match the fighting power of Japanese troops, who were better trained, more disciplined, and better armed. One young Japanese medic, Kiyoharu Tanno, who was with a company headed toward Changsha in 1945, recorded in his diary what happened when they attacked a Chinese village during one moonless night:

> Our troops broke into one house after another and knifed the soldiers they found there. The startled Chinese fled to fields, roads, and even rooftops. In no time, without our having exchanged any fire, the enemy was wiped out.

> The fighting stopped at dawn. We took a short rest to observe conditions. Some of us went toward a nearby farmhouse to look for something to use in preparing food. Suddenly a

Famine in the Midst of War

THROUGHOUT HISTORY CHINA HAS experienced many floods and famines. In 1943, during World War II, one of the worst droughts caused widespread famine in Hunan Province in northern China. The population was devastated. As crops failed and the famine went on, Chiang Kai-shek's government continued, as it had from the start, to demand taxes from the peasants. They had to pay a percentage of the grain they produced to the government. Journalist Theodore H. White, who traveled to Hunan during the 1940s to see the horrible conditions himself, reported "peasants who were eating elm bark and dried leaves had to haul their last sack of seed grain to the tax collector's office. Peasants who were so weak they could barely walk had to collect fodder [food] for the army's horses, fodder that was more nourishing than the filth they were cramming into their own mouths."

White found dead and near-dead peasants along the roadside and in gutters. Starving children were abandoned. Some people were so desperate they resorted to cannibalism. The Nationalist government ignored such reports. Local officials sold the grain that was collected and kept the profits. An estimated 2 to 3 million people died in the famine. That same number became refugees in other provinces where they searched and begged for food.

hand grenade was hurled out. . . . And we started hand-to-hand fighting with a group of Chinese. Fortunately, they were unarmed; and the hand grenade had been only a wooden dummy. One by one, we knifed the men. The skirmish ended together with their cries. . . . Some of the Chinese soldiers who fled to the fields were captured. Most of them were either shot or killed in hand-to-hand combat. Their bodies are piled up in mountainous heaps.

In April 1945, Harry S. Truman, who had been vice president under Roosevelt, became president when Roosevelt died. In July of that same year, Truman met in Potsdam, Germany, with British prime minister Winston Churchill and Soviet leader Joseph Stalin. The three leaders discussed how to deal with defeated Germany and establish postwar order. At the meeting, Truman received the news that an atomic (nuclear) bomb had been successfully tested in Alamogordo, New Mexico. The nuclear bomb had been developed in the United States during years of secret scientific work. The three leaders were confident that the threat of the bomb would bring an end to the war in a very short time. They agreed that a declaration of this news should be issued to Japan.

Later that month, on July 26, 1945, the Potsdam Declaration demanded that Japan surrender or face destruction. Japan ignored the demand. So on August 6, 1945, a U.S. bomber, the *Enola Gay*, dropped an atomic bomb on Hiroshima, Japan. It was the first nuclear device used against humans in world history. Within 75 seconds, it vaporized the city. Here is how one Japanese survivor remembers the explosion:

Suddenly a tremendous cracking sound nearly split my eardrums. A pale blue flash temporarily blinded me; then total darkness enveloped everything. When the light once again

HIROSHIMA, JAPAN, LIES IN RUINS AFTER THE ATOMIC BOMBING ON AUGUST 6, 1945. JAPAN SURRENDERED EIGHT DAYS LATER.

penetrated the blackness, I saw the city of Hiroshima reduced to ruins. . . .

Fire now raged everywhere. A black rain fell . . . smoke hid the sun. As we made our way to the Kyobashi River, whirlwinds tossed sheets of scorched . . . iron along the streets. . . . One whirlwind followed another raising clouds of sand that lashed at my back like countless needles . . . the heat was so great that we were forced to enter the water.

Despite the nuclear horror, the Japanese did not lay down their arms. Three days later, on August 9, the United States dropped a second atomic bomb on Japan, this time on Nagasaki. Finally, Japan surrendered on August 14, 1945, and World War II came to an end.

The formal surrender ceremony took place on September 2, 1945, onboard the battleship USS *Missouri*. The *Missouri* and other U.S. and British ships were anchored in Tokyo Bay, off the east coast of Japan.

Japan's defeat in World War II also ended the war between China and Japan. A broken nation, Japan no longer threatened China or any of its neighbors. But peace was not in China's immediate future. The fight between the Communists and Nationalists was about to resume, with control of China the ultimate prize.

TO SAVE FACE, JAPANESE SOLDIERS SURRENDER THEIR ARMS IN MANCHURIA IN 1945 TO RUSSIAN RATHER THAN CHINESE TROOPS.

CIVIL WAR—AGAIN

Before the end of World War II in 1945, Communist leader Zhou Enlai was certain that Chiang was spreading propaganda against the Communists and attempting to "frighten the people so that he may have a free hand in unleashing civil war and continuing his dictatorship." Zhou wrote to Communist Party leaders:

> In order to expose Chiang Kai-shek's scheme, we should concentrate on propagating [spreading] the four slogans against civil war, against dictatorship, for peace and for democracy. On specific issues, we should emphasize our right to disarm the Japanese. . . whom we have already encircled. We should point out that for the last five or six years Chiang Kai-shek has refused to recognize the armed forces of the Liberated Areas or to send them supplies and that he has not been in command of them. . . . Should the Supreme Commander of the Allied Forces arbitrarily order the Japanese troops to surrender only to Chiang's army and not to ours, it would be tantamount [the same as] to aiding Chiang to unleash a civil war, and we would firmly oppose it.

The U.S. supreme commander, General of the Army Douglas MacArthur, did indeed instruct the Japanese to surrender only to the Nationalists. To assure such an outcome, U.S. cargo planes and ships carried thousands of Chiang's troops to key areas in northern and eastern China. They were supported by two U.S. Marine divisions. The Japanese agreed to surrender to the Nationalists. As a result, the Nationalist government controlled much of East, Central, and South China.

The Communists, however, did not give up. As Communist leader Mao declared:

> Chiang Kaishek has monopolized [controlled] the right to accept the [Japanese] surrender, and for the time being . . .

the big cities and important lines of communication will not be in our hands. Nevertheless, in northern China we should still fight hard, fight with all our might to take all we can . . . our army has recovered fifty-nine cities of various sizes and vast rural areas, and including those already in our hands we now control 175 cities, thus winning a great victory.

In October 1945, Mao attended talks between Communists and Nationalists in Chongqing. Afterward he returned to headquarters in Yenan, where he reported to party members:

The Kuomintang [Nationalist Party] has accepted the principles of peace and unity, recognized certain democratic rights of the people and agreed that civil war should be averted and that the two parties should co-operate in peace to build a

> *"Why does the Kuomintang mobilize so many troops to attack us? Because long ago it made up its mind to wipe out the people's forces, to wipe us out."*
>
> —Mao Zedong, 1945

new China. . . . The Kuomintang is negotiating with us on the one hand, and is vigorously attacking the Liberated Areas on the other hand. . . . Why does the Kuomintang mobilize so many troops to attack us? Because long ago it made up its mind to wipe out the people's forces, to wipe us out. Best of all, it would like to wipe us out quickly or, failing that, to

GENERAL GEORGE C. MARSHALL, SECOND FROM LEFT, WAS SENT TO CHINA IN 1945 BY U.S. PRESIDENT HARRY TRUMAN TO NEGOTIATE AN AGREEMENT BETWEEN THE NATIONALISTS AND THE COMMUNISTS.

worsen our situation and improve its own. Peace . . . has not in fact been realized.

Certainly there was no peace. The Nationalists staged armed offensives against villages formerly loyal to the Communists (which Mao called "Liberated Areas"). The Nationalists hoped to gain control along the northern plains of China. The Communists fought for the right to their northern strongholds and territory that they had won from the Japanese.

In the midst of the fighting, U.S. president Truman sent his envoy General George C. Marshall to China. Marshall was instructed to help the Nationalists regain some authority but not to provide unrestricted support as had been previous U.S. policy. The U.S. government actually was in an odd position. It was trying to act as a peacemaker, although in the past, it had favored only one side.

Marshall hoped to negotiate an end to hostilities. When he arrived in China in December 1945, he proposed specific actions: arrange a cease-fire in the civil war; hold a conference to discuss a new government; and create a national army made up of Nationalist and Communist forces.

In January 1946, the conference brought together representatives of the Nationalists, Communists, and Democratic League (a party that held positions midway between the other two) as well as nonpartisans (people not linked to any party). Participants agreed to establish an acting government made up of multiple parties. They also settled on a cease-fire and agreed to integrate Communist troops into the national army.

However, both sides were suspicious of the U.S. role in their affairs. They also distrusted each other. After Marshall returned to the United States in March 1946, the agreement between the Nationalists and Communists fell apart. The two sides went back to their postrevolution positions. Each wanted control of the country and claimed to be the only ones fit to govern.

CHAPTER 7

The Rise of the "New China"

I N THE AFTERMATH of the 1911 revolution that brought down the ruling Qing dynasty, China suffered decades of internal strife and warfare. The hoped-for peace and prosperity did not take place. China splintered into many factions, each with different and often conflicting goals. Ultimately, the struggle for China came down to two factions: the Nationalists led by Chiang Kai-shek and the Communists led by Mao Zedong. In the wake of the revolution, the Nationalists had steadily gained power but ultimately lost the support of the people. The Communists, on the other hand, lacked the influence of the Nationalists in both internal and world affairs. But the Communists had spent years building goodwill and support among the Chinese people—especially the millions of peasants living in rural areas.

With the end of World War II, the Communists' moment in history had arrived. Mao envisioned a "New China"—a China that, in his words, would be a nation in which the people would "educate and remould themselves on a country-wide scale by democratic methods and, with everyone taking part, shake off the influence of domestic and foreign reactionaries [anti-Communists] . . . rid themselves of the bad habits and ideas acquired in the old society . . . and continue to advance—advance towards a socialist and communist society."

Mao proclaimed this New China in 1949. In that year, the People's Republic of China was born.

THE COMMUNIST BUILDUP

By the time that China's long civil war was coming to an end, the Communists had built their troops to more than 1.5 million (some sources say up to 2 million) soldiers. They had renamed their military forces the People's Liberation Army (PLA). Although the Nationalists had more troops, money, equipment, and supplies than the Communists, the PLA used more effective guerrilla strikes to stop the Nationalists. Another tactic was to isolate Nationalist forces by surrounding them, cutting off communication and supplies, and then attacking.

FAST FACT

BY ABOUT 1949, THE PEOPLE'S LIBERATION ARMY HAD ABOUT 1.5 MILLION TO 2 MILLION SOLDIERS.

The Communists gained advantage over the Nationalists for other reasons as well. They were far more successful than the Nationalists at winning public support. When the Communists took control of a region, particularly in rural areas, they introduced land reforms. In Manchuria, for example, they took over estates that had been occupied by the Japanese and turned plots over to peasants. In some cases, women benefited from

LED BY MAO ZEDONG, RIGHT, THE COMMUNIST TROOPS, ABOVE,
WERE FAR MORE SUCCESSFUL AT WINNING PUBLIC SUPPORT THAN
THE NATIONALISTS.

land reform. Traditionally, they had not been allowed to own land.
When they did receive a share of redistributed land, they tended to join
the Communists. Another motivation was the Communists' support
of a woman's right to divorce her husband and gain custody of their
children. For centuries in China, only men were allowed to ask for a
divorce. After a divorce, children had to remain with their fathers.

The Nationalists were established in the coastal regions far from
the countryside and farming areas. The Nationalist government had

little understanding of the problems peasants faced. It "was unsympathetic to their cause . . . and looked down upon the peasants as an inert [slow moving] entity. They failed to see the revolutionary potential of the peasant masses and consequently never attempted to organize them," according to historian Immanuel C.Y. Hsu.

A FAILED GOVERNMENT

The Nationalists had actually started losing public support even before the end of World War II. The government was seen as cor-

U.S. AMBASSADOR JOHN L. STUART, RIGHT, MEETS WITH CHIANG KAI-SHEK IN 1946. STUART OFTEN CRITICIZED THE NATIONALIST GOVERNMENT FOR ITS MANY FAILINGS.

rupt and incompetent. Madame Sun Yat-sen, wife of the deceased revolutionary and Nationalist leader, was convinced that Chiang was preparing for another civil war. She complained bitterly and contemptuously to British war correspondent Stuart Gelder in 1944. She told him that Chiang's government was a dictatorial tyranny, not the democracy that her husband had envisioned. Chiang, she said, "has not even attempted to put one of my husband's principles into operation." She said that she had expressed her opinions to Chiang, but he then refused to speak to her again.

After World War II, reports coming out of China from journalists, historians, and U.S. officials also criticized the Nationalist government and its failings. A typical criticism came from U.S. ambassador and missionary John L. Stuart. Although Stuart had many friends among the Nationalists, he wrote that

> this party almost from the time it came into power had tolerated among its officials of all grades graft [theft] and greed, idleness and inefficiency, nepotism [benefits given to family members] and factional rivalries [disagreements]—all the evils . . . of the corrupt bureaucracy it had overthrown. These evils had become more pronounced after V-J Day [Victory over Japan Day] in the attempts to crush Communism by a combination of military strength and secret police. The government had been steadily losing support and even respect.

Other critics blasted Chiang for such problems as police brutality and repression. High taxes and unfair collection of revenue were major concerns as well. While most citizens paid the required taxes, a small group of influential people paid nothing. In some cases, they even benefited from tax monies paid by their fellow citizens. The four wealthiest families in China—the Chiangs, Soongs, Kongs, and

Chens—were known as the Big Four Families. They ran most of the country's largest businesses, and even whole industries. Members of these families also held high rank in the Nationalist army. They "controlled virtually every element of Nationalist China life through government monopolies. They were taking millions of dollars for themselves each month" wrote foreign correspondent Edwin P. Hoyt. "On the military level the generals were taking the money for their armies and using it for themselves. On the civil level the officials found it impossible to live on their salaries because of inflation, so they turned to all sorts of corrupt practices. Bribery was so common that it did not cause a raised eyebrow."

Corruption and overall mismanagement of the economy led to serious economic problems. For instance, the government needed money, so it simply printed as much currency as it wanted. As a result, the value of the yuan fell steadily. To illustrate the problem, a political cartoon showed the declining value of the yuan by what it could buy: In 1939 the yuan would purchase a pig, in 1941 a sack of flour, in 1943 a chicken, in 1945 two eggs, in 1947 a piece of coal, and in 1949 only a sheet of paper.

On August 19, 1948, the Nationalist government issued a new currency called the gold yuan. People were forced to turn in their old yuan for the new paper money. In addition, everyone was required to exchange whatever U.S. dollars, silver, and gold they had for the gold yuan. If individuals and businesses did not go along, they could be and were executed. As the government printed more and more paper money, the value of the Chinese currency continued to fall. Eventually the new yuan was almost as worthless as the old. "Inflation and financial mismanagement destroyed the livelihood of hundreds of millions of Chinese and totally discredited the government," wrote historian Hsu.

SOLDIERS IN THE NATIONALIST ARMY

Nationalist Army troops also turned against the government during the years following the end of World War II. Many were poorly paid or not paid at all, and some suffered mistreatment by officers. Many, including those captured by the PLA, deserted and went over to the Communist side.

Journalists such as Jack Belden, who reported from China before and after World War II, and New York *Time-Life* war correspondents Theodore H. White and Annalee Jacoby wrote highly critical reports of the Nationalist army under Chiang. They wrote of soldiers who were treated badly, who were thought to be profoundly ignorant, who were treated more like "dumb beasts" than people. Officers frequently beat soldiers with bamboo rods or other items. Belden noted that "the life of the ordinary soldier was but one cut above a

NATIONALIST TROOPS HOLD A POSITION IN MANCHURIA IN 1946 AGAINST THE COMMUNISTS. SOME NATIONALIST TROOPS WERE TREATED BADLY BY THEIR COMMANDERS.

pig and a cut below a mule. As a matter of fact, mules, on the whole, were better fed and better cared for than men."

White also reported harsh treatment. "Soldiers could be beaten, even killed, at a commander's whim, and punishment included ear-cropping and flogging . . . a soldier might be punished by being made to kneel on his bare knees on a rocky parade ground, with his hands bound behind his back, until he collapsed in the burning sun."

"Doomed men" is what White called Nationalist soldiers. Millions lost their lives in battles. Countless more died of diseases such as malaria and tuberculosis, infections, starvation, and exhaustion. It was a wonder that the army could fight at all let alone win on the battlefield. "The army's greatest victory was its staying alive and withstanding the disintegrating pressure of its own government and society," White wrote.

THE RED ARMY

Unlike Nationalist forces, Communist soldiers were well disciplined. Their morale was high in spite of many physical hardships. From the early days of the Red Army in the 1920s and 1930s, soldiers believed they were fighting for a worthy cause. Edgar Snow, the American journalist who was the first Westerner to interview Mao and publish the Communist leader's autobiographical account, observed the Red troops in 1936. In his book *Red Star over China,* Snow describes the daily life of Red soldiers:

> [They] were quartered in caves, former stables of wealthy land-lords, hastily erected barracks of clay and wood, and in com-pounds and houses abandoned by former officials or garrison troops . . . rooms were fairly neat, clean, and orderly. . . . They seldom had tables or desks, and piles of bricks or rocks served

as chairs, most of the furniture having been destroyed or carted off by the enemy before his retreat.

The Red soldier, when not fighting, had a full and busy day. In the Northwest, as in the South, he had long periods of military inactivity, for when a new district was occupied, the Red Army settled down for a month or two to establish soviets and otherwise "consolidate," and only put a small force on outpost duty. . . .

When not in the trenches or on outpost duty, the red soldier observed a six-day week. He arose at five and retired to a "Taps" sounded at nine. The schedule of the day included: an hour's exercise immediately after rising; breakfast; two hours of military drill; two hours of political lectures and discussion; lunch; an hour of rest; two hours of character study; two hours of games and sports; dinner; songs and group meetings; and "Taps."

Snow also wrote that he was impressed with the soldiers' competitive nature and their agility. They took part in "broad jumping, high jumping, running, wall scaling, rope climbing, grenade throwing, and marksmanship," he reported.

Training and discipline of the Red troops continued throughout the 1940s, World War II, and beyond. The Communists succeeded in gaining converts and territory. Mao Zedong has been credited with much of the Communist expansion.

WHY COMMUNISTS WERE VICTORIOUS

Various historians, war correspondents, and other observers have spelled out some of the reasons that the Communists were able to claim victory over the Nationalists. Indian correspondent Frank Moraes, who interviewed Chiang in 1944 while he was still in power, placed blame on the generalissimo himself.

As Moraes explains, "Chiang failed because he believed primarily and entirely in himself. He was China. In his cold, complex calculations he overlooked one small item. He forgot the Chinese people. He believed that he and he alone could lift them by their bootstraps to bigger things. . . . Between his government and his people yawned a gap which grew wider with the years." Moraes concludes that democracy had not failed, "for Chiang's government was never a democracy" but instead a government run by only a few people. "Sun Yat-sen's Three Principles stood. But the men who carried his banner had fallen by the wayside."

> *"Chiang failed because he believed primarily and entirely in himself...In his cold, complex calculations he overlooked one small item. He forgot the Chinese people."*
>
> —Frank Moraes, Indian journalist, 1944

In *The Cambridge Illustrated History of China*, Patricia Buckley Ebrey points out: "The more scholars uncover about life in the 1930s and 1940s [in China], the more failings of the Nationalists they find: widespread government corruption, spiraling inflation, intractable [not easily eliminated] poverty, the alienation of the educated elite, the presence of warlordism, and so on." As for the Communists, they

**COMMUNIST TROOPS, ABOVE IN 1946, WERE BETTER ORGANIZED AND
EQUIPPED THAN THEIR NATIONALIST COUNTERPARTS.**

were better organized than their rivals. Even when the Japanese invaded, the Communists worked behind the lines and kept their bases. The opposite was true of Chiang and his forces, many of whom were scattered in outlying areas beyond Nationalist strongholds.

The Communists also won the loyalty of workers, students, and peasants. People joined the Communists out of "patriotism or on a revolutionary impulse, or through a combination of both reasons," according to historian Jacques Guillermaz. Although the Communist party was by no means a democracy in the sense that Western nations understand the term, it promoted ideals of equality and justice.

However, these ideals fell by the wayside as the party gained power and control over the people.

MAO'S RISE TO POWER

After Mao established Communist headquarters in Yenan, Shaanxi Province, his position in the CCP from the 1930s to the 1940s was in constant flux. Sometimes he held leadership posts. Other times he was out of favor with the party.

While in Yenan, Mao urged party members to empathize with the peasants by working, living, and eating with them. Communists conducted land reforms and rent reduction programs, involving peasants and farm labor unions. Mao also created a system of government

U.S. OFFICERS MEET WITH MAO, SECOND FROM LEFT, AND ZHOU ENLAI, RIGHT, AT THE YENAN CONFERENCE IN AUGUST 1945 TO TRY AND REACH AN AGREEMENT BETWEEN COMMUNIST AND NATIONALIST FORCES.

in which only one-third of posts could be filled by party members. Citizens and intellectuals made up two-thirds of the local government. With such political maneuvers, constant propaganda, and deadly Red Army attacks on the KMT, Mao and the Communists managed to build loyalty to their cause and undermine the Nationalist government.

When war correspondent White was in northern China in 1944, he went to Yenan, which had a population of thirty thousand. He visited the Communist headquarters, which included two groups of buildings—one for leaders of the party and the other for the army. White reported that party leaders "agitated, trained, and molded the 12,000-odd party members who lived and worked in caves that studded the slopes of the hills for miles about the town."

White describes the party leaders as having a "sense of unity" and being cocky and arrogant at times. But for the most part, they lived simply. For example,

> officials and party members were expected to cultivate land in order to raise their own food and lift the burden of their support from the local peasants . . . the party and its function-aries lived not on taxes but on the sweat of their own brow. Mao Tse-tung tended a tobacco patch . . . and raised enough [tobacco] for all party headquarters. Chu Teh [Zhu De], the commander in chief, grew cabbages.

The party leaders, White found, were "engineers of social rela-tionships . . . knew precisely what the peasants' grievances were and precisely how those grievances could be transmuted [turned into] ac-tion." They were able to put Communist ideas into language that the "most illiterate peasant could understand and accept as his own."

Mao began to sense in late 1947 that he and his Red Army would gain power. In a manifesto issued in October, he wrote that Chiang's "twenty-year rule has been traitorous, dictatorial and against the people." Mao called for the overthrow of Chiang and spelled out the basic policies of the Red Army. These included uniting the people and forming a democratic coalition government; arresting and punishing Chiang and others labeled "civil war criminals;" destroying Chiang's

The 228 Incident in Taiwan

IN 1885 THE ISLAND of Taiwan, with a population of immigrants from mainland China and indigenous local groups, became a province of China. China lost the province in a war with Japan, and the Japanese ruled Taiwan from 1895 to 1945. During World War II, the Japanese used the island as a base of operations. After their surrender, the Nationalist government occupied Taiwan, claiming to "liberate" it.

However, just the opposite occurred. The new authorities dealt with the Chinese in Taiwan "as enemy collaborators; their goods were seized and the economy despoiled [looted] by Nationalist military and politicians seeking personal loot," according to the late John King Fairbank, director of the East Asian Research Center at Harvard. Repression and corruption became progressively worse. By February 1947, a brutal incident led to a large-scale public demonstration against the government.

On February 28, a woman was arrested for selling smuggled cigarettes on the street, a common practice. She resisted, and the arresting officer hit her on the head with his rifle, killing her. Unarmed protestors gathered and police shot into the crowd. One person was killed and others were wounded. The day became known as the 228 Incident, which stood for February, the second month, and the twenty-eighth day of the month.

Protests continued for more than a week. On the mainland, Chiang sent KMT troops to put down the revolt. An estimated eight thousand to ten thousand Taiwanese were killed. From that time on, Chiang declared martial law and brutally repressed any opposition, especially after he fled to Taiwan in 1949 and became a dictatorial ruler.

dictatorship; getting rid of corrupt government officials; confiscating the property of the Big Four families; instituting land reform; and rejecting Chiang's foreign policy and negotiating fair treaties with foreign countries. These were part of the terms for a Nationalist surrender in 1949.

As the Nationalists were losing control, Mao held a series of meetings with delegates to a national conference. There he was elected chairman of the Central Committee of the CCP. At one gathering on September 21, 1949, he declared in his opening address that the conference was "representative of the people of the whole country and enjoys their trust and support." Mao told more than six hundred delegates that their "work will go down in the history of mankind, demonstrating that the Chinese people, comprising one quarter of humanity, have now stood up." It was a declaration that the People's Republic of China had been established. It also demonstrated that a Communist revolution had been accomplished with peasants and guerrillas in the countryside along with the proletariat in industrial cities.

Chiang and his Nationalist forces fled to Taiwan, an island off the southeastern coast of China. Japan had taken over Taiwan from China in 1895, and during World War II, the Japanese used the island to stage attacks in the Pacific. After the Japanese surrender, Taiwan was given to the Nationalist government on China's mainland.

When Chiang escaped to Taiwan, he took with him the entire gold reserves of China. About 2 million Nationalist refugees and soldiers left the mainland for the island. There Chiang set up a Nationalist government, with Taipei as its capital. Chiang claimed until the day he died on April 5, 1975, that the Nationalist Party was the legitimate government of China.

A little more than a week after his election as CCP chairman, Mao Zedong appeared in Tiananmen Square. On October 1, 1949, he publicly announced the formation of a "new China." Many citizens believed that meant the struggles and bloodshed in the aftermath of the 1911 revolution were not in vain and that a democratic government would be forthcoming. "We thought China was going to be a fair world forever," noted Zhao Youping, who was in Tiananmen Square on the day Mao made his announcement. Organized KMT forces were not engaged in battles as they had been in the years following the 1911 revolution. But small groups attempted to resist the Communists. In less than a decade, however, Mao and the Communists forcefully put down "reactionaries" and "revisionists"— people opposed to or thought to be against Communism. Using smart political tactics to organize peasants and workers and brutally maintaining control, Mao gained absolute power. He became a ruthless dictator, ruling the country until his death in 1976.

A FTER THE COMMUNISTS established the People's Republic of China in 1949, about eight or nine years of peace
and social and economic order began. It was a period that both the
Communists and Nationalists had fought for during the turmoil after
the 1911 revolution. The public believed that the CCP, with Mao at
the helm, would get rid of warlords, abolish foreign influence, elimi-
nate corruption, and modernize China. Because of all the upheaval
in the aftermath of the revolution, China's economy had fallen far
behind the rest of the world's industrialized countries.

Beginning in 1958, one government program after another was
created to build a new society with state-controlled agricultural and
industrial production. The programs, however, failed to improve
China's economy. Mao also started programs to get the Chinese
people to accept Communist ideas. This was particularly true during
his Great Proletarian Cultural Revolution (1966–1976), when almost
every aspect of life in China was at its most unstable. The purpose
of the Cultural Revolution was to bring about a classless society in
which all people shared the same social and economic status. Under
Mao's dictatorship, past customs, ideas, and habits were criticized
and eliminated. Mao formed a Red Guard of young people who
destroyed furniture, jewelry, books, art objects, musical instruments,
and other items reflecting high social status or wealth. People were
expected to live by the Cultural Revolution slogan that it was "better to be poor under socialism than rich under capitalism." Anyone
who did not go along with the Party line was punished—humiliated
in public, beaten, or killed. Those who had their doubts did not

dare speak out. Even Mao's personal physician of twenty-two years, Li Zhisui, could not object to anything the dictator said or did. "Those of us around him had to grant his every wish," Li wrote in his memoir.

Nevertheless, there were power struggles within the CCP. Leaders differed on whether Mao's policies should be continued or moderated. After Mao's death in 1976, some leaders criticized Mao's ideas. One who did this was Deng Xiaoping, vice-chairman of the CCP and chief of the general staff of the People's Liberation Army. Deng argued for economic reform and publicly rejected some of Mao's theories about a classless society. In 1978, under Deng's direction, the Central Committee of the CCP adopted economic reforms called the Four Modernizations. According to the plan, agriculture, industry, the military, and science and technology would be updated to help create a modern China. Deng referred to the reforms as "socialism with Chinese characteristics." By that he meant that socialism would be designed to fit Chinese conditions. He further explained that socialism would advance to communism based on the ideal,

> from each according to his ability and to each according to his needs. . . . This calls for highly developed productive forces and an overwhelming abundance of material wealth. Therefore, the fundamental task for the socialist stage is to develop the productive forces. . . . As they develop, the people's material and cultural life will constantly improve.

Reformers like Deng wanted to establish a modern economic system. That system, they believed, should include elements of capitalism, in which some private citizens would be allowed to produce goods, sell them, and earn profits.

Under the leadership of Deng, China slowly made reforms. It embraced some capitalist ideas while maintaining a Socialist system

MASSIVE DEMONSTRATIONS, SUCH AS THIS ONE IN TIANANMEN SQUARE IN THE LATE 1960s, WERE PART OF MAO'S CULTURAL REVOLUTION, WHICH SOUGHT TO CREATE A CLASSLESS SOCIETY IN CHINA.

that included both state ownership and collective ownership of property and business. New rail lines, steel mills, and oil pipelines were built. Educational systems that had been neglected or closed down under Mao were revived. Deng knew that China needed technology and investment, and he offered tax incentives for foreign companies to set up businesses in China. Agriculture also developed with the increased use of mechanized farm equipment. The standard of living for many Chinese improved. People were able to earn enough money to buy the goods they needed.

Yet over the decades, the CCP maintained absolute political control. The government still muffled dissent, as was evident with the much-publicized events in Tiananmen Square in 1989. In the spring of that year, university students called for increased political reforms such as freedom of expression. They staged hunger strikes and protest marches. Deng declared martial law and demanded that students and others leave Tiananmen Square on June 3 and June 4. When army troops with tanks were ordered to clear out the protestors, as many as three thousand citizens were killed while TV cameras rolled. Viewers around the world watched in horror.

Many witnesses to the massacre became disillusioned with their government, but others were more concerned about the economic development of their country. In 2005 reporters with the British

A LONE STUDENT DEMONSTRATOR BRAVELY CONFRONTS A LINE OF CHINESE ARMY TANKS DURING THE TIANANMEN SQUARE DEMONSTRATIONS IN 1989.

Broadcasting Company (BBC) found that numerous students interviewed were not protesting for an ideal. Rather, as one student said, "I think many young people like me pay less attention to politics, and more attention to living better and economic improvement. They don't care about politics in China." Teng Jimeng, a professor at Beijing Foreign Studies University, agreed, saying "this is the most apathetic and indifferent generation China has ever produced." Teng called the situation "unprecedented in Chinese history. The general level of people's living standards is greatly improved and with the economy doing so very well, people feel satisfied and pacified."

China in the twenty-first century is a powerful player on the global economic stage. Predictions for what the future holds for China vary greatly. On the one hand, many new worries are surfacing. The environment is one big concern. Air and water pollution caused by more cars and growth in manufacturing are on the rise in China. On the other hand, China has unlimited potential. "China, with the world's largest population and fastest growing economy, is in a rapid transition from the status of a developing to a developed country," as John Gittings, China specialist for the British *Guardian*, wrote. A "new 'New China'" certainly is emerging, and it had its start almost a century ago with a rebellion against the old order.

Timeline

1911 The republican revolution breaks out in Hubei Province on October 10.

1912 Sun Yat-sen becomes the provisional president of thenew Chinese republic in January. The Manchu emperor, the child Puyi, abdicates in February. Sun resigns, and Yuan Shikai becomes the provisional president of the Republic of China. The Kuomintang (KMT) or Nationalist Party is founded.

1913 Seven southern provinces rebel against Yuan.

1914 World War I erupts in Europe. Japan joins the Allies against Germany and seizes German properties and naval bases in China.

1915 Yuan announces the establishment of a new monarchy, and widespread uprisings follow. Japan presents China with "Twenty-one Demands."

1916 Yuan dies.

1917 China declares war on Germany.

1919 Student protests on May 4 mark the beginning of the May Fourth Movement. Sun Yat-sen reestablishes the KMT.

1921 Sun seeks and obtains support from the Soviet Union.

1925 Sun dies. Chiang Kai-shek begins the Northern Expedition against the warlords.

1926 The KMT splits into two factions. One faction is led by Chiang. The other faction favors the Chinese Communist Party.

1927 Mao Zedong launches the Autumn Harvest Uprising among the peasants, which fails.

1928 Chiang controls all of China. Civil war erupts between the Communists and Nationalists.

1931 Mao establishes a soviet in Jiangxi Province. Japan seizes Manchuria and continues its aggression against China.

1934–1935 From October 1934 to October 1935, the Red Army undertakes the Long March to escape Chiang's forces. The survivors establish a soviet in Shaanxi Province.

1936 Chiang is kidnapped by rebellious KMT troops.

1937 The Second United Front against Japan begins.

1938 The alliance between the Nationalists and Communists shatters.

1939 World War II begins in Europe.

1941 Japan bombs the U.S. Navy base at Pearl Harbor, Hawaii. The United States declares war.

1942 General Joseph W. Stilwell takes charge of America's China-Burma-India military operations.

1943 The United States and Britain end their unequal treaty relations with China.

1945 President Harry Truman orders a war plane to drop atomic bombs on Hiroshima and Nagasaki, Japan. World War II ends.

1945–1949 China's civil war is in its last stages.

1949 The civil war ends. Mao proclaims the People's Republic of China.

1966 Mao's ten-year Cultural Revolution begins.

1976 Mao dies.

1978 Deng Xiaoping, vice chairman of the CCP, adopts economic reforms in China.

1989 China's security forces kill thousands of protestors in Tiananmen Square.

Glossary

bourgeoisie: in Communist theory, the middle class, often made up of merchants and owners of small businesses

Chinese Communist Party (CCP): the political party led by Mao Zedong that proclaimed the People's Republic of China in 1949

coalition: an alliance

Comintern: an international organization sponsored by the Soviet Union to spread Communist ideas worldwide

constitutional democracy: a governmental system based on a constitution that establishes the makeup and powers of government

guerrillas: armed forces who are not part of a regular military but engage in hit-and-run warfare in small units

Kuomintang or Guomindang Party (KMT): the Nationalist Party founded in 1912 by Sun Yat-sen and later led by Chiang Kai-shek

Long March: a year-long trek (1934–1935) of Chinese Communists through remote areas of western China to escape Nationalist forces

militia: a citizen army rather than a professional military force

monarchy: a government ruled by a monarch—a king or emperor who inherits the title

Opium Wars: wars in the 1800s fought first between China and Britain and later between China and a British-French alliance because Great Britain forced China to accept imports of opium

People's Liberation Army (PLA): one of the largest military forces in the world. It traces its roots to the 1927 uprising of the Chinese Communists against the Nationalists.

proletariat: in Communist theory, workers or the working class

Qing (Ching) dynasty: the last imperial dynasty, founded by the Manchu, to rule China (1644–1912)

regent: a person who acts on behalf of the state when the ruler is a minor, incapacitated, or absent

right of extraterritoriality: the right to be immune from local laws while in a foreign nation

secede: the act of withdrawing

spheres of influence: a nation's control over a territory in a foreign country

Tiananmen Square: a public square at the center of Beijing where numerous protests and other gatherings have taken place

Treaty of Versailles: an agreement ending World War I and signed in 1919 at the Palace of Versailles near Paris, France

warlords: Chinese generals who controlled provinces or other local territories

Who's Who?

Otto Braun (1900–1974): A German Communist, Braun called himself Li De in Chinese. The international Comintern, which was established by the Soviet Union to spread communism in other countries, sent Braun to China. His mission was to provide military advice for the Red Army, which was fighting Chiang Kai-shek's Kuomintang forces in a civil war.

Braun intended to be a teacher and attended a teacher's training school in Pasing, Germany. During World War I, he was drafted into the Bavarian army but was not in any armed conflict. Although he completed teachers' training, he did not teach but chose to travel around Germany.

He was active with the German Communist Party in the early 1920s and became the leader of its counterintelligence service. He spent time in prison for his espionage work and escaped to Moscow, where he studied at the Frunze Military Academy, graduating in 1932. The next year, he was in China and managed to reach the southern part of Jiangxi Province at Ruijin, where Mao Zedong was based. According to author Edgar Snow, Braun was "smuggled into the Red areas in a sampan [boat] where he lay covered with cargo for many days."

During the KMT's encirclement campaigns against the Red Army, Braun advised the Communist troops to follow rigid military strategy rather than use the guerrilla tactics that had been so successful for them. Braun's advice led to a major retreat for the Red Army and the Long March of 1934–1935. During the March, Braun's failed military tactics contributed to enormous losses for the Communists. Mao took over, putting Braun in a lower position.

Braun left China in 1939 and went to Moscow, where he worked for the Foreign Languages Press and as a lecturer. He returned to East Germany after Stalin's death in 1954 and worked as a writer and also as a translator of Russian publications. He died while on a holiday in Bulgaria in 1974 and was buried in East Berlin.

Chiang Kai-shek (1887–1975): Chiang (also known as Chiang Chung-cheng) was born in Zhejiang Province to a wealthy family. He attended private school, learning the classics, and went on to enroll in military school in Tokyo, Japan, which was a hub for Chinese revolutionaries. When he returned to China, he became a military aide to Sun Yat-sen, leader of the Kuomintang (KMT) or Nationalist Party.

After Sun's death, Chiang led an expedition to overthrow warlords controlling much of northern China. He became the leader of the Nationalist government in 1928. During his career, he formed an alliance with the Communists and then turned against them, launching a long civil war. His forces also took part in a war with Japan (1937–1945) while World War II was under way. After the Japanese were expelled in 1945, civil war erupted again between the Communists and the KMT. The Communists won control of the country in 1949. Chiang was forced to flee to Taiwan, where he established a Nationalist government with himself in firm control as president. He ruled as a dictator until his death in 1975.

Lin Biao or Lin Piao (ca. 1907–1971): Born in Hubei Province, Lin Biao was eighteen when he entered an officers' training school at the Huangpu (Whampoa) Military Academy in Guangzhou (Canton). He became known as a brilliant military hero by the time he was twenty-eight years old and took part in Chiang Kai-shek's Nationalist expedition to oust warlords in northern China. When Chiang turned on the Communists, Lin joined Mao Zedong's Red Army. He led guerrilla troops against the Kuomintang (or Nationalists) and is said to have been victorious in every battle. He was Mao's trusted commander, became minister of defense, and was responsible for compiling some of Mao's writings in *Quotations of Chairman Mao,* popularly called the *Little Red Book.*

Mao named Lin as his successor. But as Lin gained political power, he apparently became a threat to Mao. According to the CCP's official assessment, Lin planned to assassinate the Chairman, the plot was uncovered, and Lin with family members fled by plane to Russia in 1971. The plane crashed and all aboard were killed. Yet there is no certainty about Lin's disappearance. Some historians suspect he was executed.

Mao Zedong or Mao Tse-tung (1893–1976): Mao Zedong was one of a dozen Marxists who founded China's Communist Party (CCP) in 1921. He believed in the theories of German philosopher Karl Marx. Marx argued that throughout history people have been divided into economic classes. He believed that class struggles take place because of economics. People who control the land and means of production gain wealth and power while the proletariat (working class) has no power. Marx predicted that the proletariat would rise up against the ruling class in a revolution. He believed that revolutionon would bring about a classless society and an economic system now known as communism.

Mao was born in the village of Shaoshan, near Changsha, the capital city of Hunan Province. His family acquired land and a business, becoming rich peasants. Although his father wanted him to work on the family farm, Mao chose to do otherwise. He left home during his teenage years to go to school in Changsha and later in Peking (Beijing). He served for a brief time in the military during the 1911 revolution, but he was never in combat.

Mao was an avid reader and a prolific writer. His numerous articles, revolutionary directives to the people, speeches, and poems were published during his lifetime and after his death. Much of Mao's writing was political and reflected his increasing interest in the CCP, which in its early years was a small organization. During the first half of the 1920s, the CCP worked with the Kuomintang (KMT) Party, which was led by Chiang Kai-shek, to achieve revolutionary goals. The Soviet Union advised both the CCP and the KMT, expecting that China would be a Communist state like the USSR. But the parties differed in their methods. The CCP stressed peasant organizations, and the KMT emphasized cooperation with merchants and military leaders to establish a united government.

The CCP and KMT split in 1927 when Chiang turned on the Communists. A civil war erupted that lasted for ten years. In 1937 the CCP and KMT united once again to fight Japanese aggression in China. But civil war resumed after World War II as each party tried to gain control. Mao's use of guerrilla tactics eventually helped the Reds overcome Chiang's much larger forces, and Mao and the CCP proclaimed the People's Republic of China in 1949. From then on, Mao imposed his brand of communism on the people. Millions of Chinese died from brutal treatment under Mao's rule. He suppressed all opposition until his death in 1976.

Marshall, George C. (1880–1959): U.S. president Harry Truman called General George C. Marshall "the greatest living American" for his topmost efforts in World War II. Truman appointed Marshall U.S. ambassador in China, where the general hoped to negotiate an end to the civil war between Nationalists and Communists.

Marshall was born and grew up in Pennsylvania. He attended the Virginia Military Institute. After graduation he served in a variety of posts as a young officer, including an appointment to the general staff during World War I. In 1939, as World War II in Europe began, President Franklin Roosevelt named Marshall chief of staff of the U.S. Army. His service as a strategist was praised worldwide. Increasing global recognition came his way when he developed the European Recovery Program, later called the Marshall Plan. The plan provided millions of dollars in aid for Britain, France, and West Germany to rebuild after the war. That effort helped the countries increase their industrial production and income, which allowed them to contribute to the U.S. economy. In 1953 Marshall won the Nobel Peace Prize for his plan.

Marshall retired from military service in 1945 and began a diplomatic career. Truman sent him to China as his envoy in late 1945, but Marshall's attempt to find a peaceful settlement to the civil war failed. He returned to the United States in 1947.

Because Marshall failed to bring the two sides together, and because of the Communist takeover of China in 1949, he was criticized back home. Anti-Red groups in the United States accused him of being friendly with the Communists. Senator Joseph McCarthy, who conducted congressional hearings to identify Communists in the U.S. government, mounted one of the strongest attacks on Marshall. McCarthy's wild accusations were heard and seen on television, but he was later condemned by the Senate for inappropriate behavior.

Marshall retired from government service in 1949 but was again called back during the Korean War (1950–1953). Two years later, he retired from public and private service for the last time. He died in 1959 and was buried in Arlington National Cemetery near Washington, D.C.

Puyi (1905–1967): In 1908, when he was three years old, Puyi (or P'u-I) was named emperor of the Qing dynasty by the dowager empress. But the empress died shortly thereafter, and a regent ruled until the boy emperor came of age.

A year after the revolution of 1911, the Republic of China demanded that Puyi give up his throne. But the new government guaranteed that the boy would retain his title and income. He and his family were allowed to stay in the Forbidden City, located on Tiananmen Square in Peking (Beijing), where they lived as if they were still royalty.

Puyi grew up inside this walled city of 250 acres (11 ha) that was also surrounded by a moat. The child emperor was educated by tutors. One of his tutors was British and taught Puyi English. He also helped Puyi, at his request, pick an English name. Puyi's choice was "Henry," so he became known to Westerners as Henry Puyi, although his Chinese name was simply "Puyi."

When Puyi was a teenager, several warlords attempted to restore the dynasty and put Puyi on the throne again. Their efforts failed. Another warlord, who opposed the monarchy, forced Puyi out of the Forbidden City. It was the first time he had been outside the walls. Puyi with his family and large staff took refuge in the Japanese section of Tianjin, a busy city with many foreign diplomatic centers.

After the Japanese occupied Manchuria in 1931, they renamed it Manchukuo and set up Puyi as emperor. At the end of World War II, the Soviets took over Manchuria. When the People's Republic of China was established in 1949, Mao requested that Puyi be sent back to China. There he was imprisoned, forced to adopt Mao's ideas, and voice support for communism. He was released in 1959, and during the early 1960s worked as a common gardener, was appointed to various political committees, and wrote his autobiography. He died of cancer in 1967.

Stalin, Joseph (1879–1953): Not long after declaring the People's Republic of China (PRC), Mao Zedong declared that the nation would follow the pattern of Russia's Union of Soviet Socialist Republics (USSR). The Soviet Union had recognized the PRC in 1949. Mao met with the Soviet Union's dictator Joseph Stalin to seek loans and advisers to help set up Chinese industries. Stalin and Mao signed a Treaty of Friendship, Alliance, and Mutual Assistance in 1950, which provided the requested money and technicians for China.

Born in Gori, Georgia, Joseph Stalin was one of four children, but his three siblings died. He was in poor health during his childhood. Although his parents were poor, his mother was able to enroll him in a religious school. He did well in his studies but was said to have been expelled because he tried to convince students to accept socialism. While a young man, he changed his original name (Iosif Vissarionovich Dzhugashvili) to Stalin, meaning "Man of Steel."

Stalin became a member of the Social Democratic Labor Party in 1901 and organized strikes and resistance to the czar. He was arrested, imprisoned, and sent to Siberia. He escaped and continued his organizing. Four more times he was imprisoned and escaped.

Over the years, Stalin's revolutionary and party activities led to his rise in power. He eventually became dictator of the Soviet Union. His regime became known as terror ridden and murderous—millions died under his rule. Yet, he played a major role in the defeat of Nazi Germany during World War II.

Stalin's ruthless dictatorship lasted for twenty-five years. He died of a stroke in 1953.

Stilwell, Joseph W. (1883–1946): Known as "Vinegar Joe" because of his sharp, no-nonsense style, General Joseph Stilwell was commander of U.S. Army forces in the China-Burma-India (CBI) theater during World War II. He also was Generalissimo Chiang Kai-shek's chief of staff. His job was to train KMT troops and hold Chinese bases against Japan's aggression.

Stilwell was born in Florida and raised in Yonkers, New York. He enrolled in the U.S. Military Academy at West Point in New York when he was eighteen years old and served in France during World War I. After the war, he went to Bejing to study and learn the Chinese language. He served as a military attaché at the U.S. embassy in China for a time, then returned to the United States to teach military tactics.

In 1942, after the United States had entered World War II, President Franklin Roosevelt sent Stilwell to China to aid the Nationalist Army. But Chiang Kai-shek and Stilwell did not get along. Chiang considered Stilwell arrogant and harsh. Stilwell called Chiang a "peanut" and declared his tactics were cowardly and irrational. The two also were divided by their ideas. Stilwell was convinced that the Nationalists and Communists should unite to fight the Japanese. Chiang wanted no part of the Red Army.

When Japan conquered Burma in 1942, Stilwell led his forces to India. There he rebuilt his army and also ordered the construction of the Ledo Road, which bypassed the portion of the famed Burma Road that the Japanese had blocked.

When Stilwell retreated into India, Chiang was displeased. In his view, it was humiliating, and the soldiers should have stayed to fight.

Stilwell believed in fighting back. Stilwell and Chiang constantly were at odds, and after two years, Chiang finally got a replacement for Stilwell, who was recalled to the United States. Stilwell went on to command forces and achieve victory in Okinawa, Japan.

In the United States, Stilwell and his family lived in California. He suffered from cancer and died in 1946 after an operation in a San Francisco hospital.

Yuan Shikai (1859–1916): A major figure in China, Yuan was a military official in the Manchu dynasty and supported Dowager Empress Cixi against the reform movement of Emperor Guangxu. He suppressed the Boxer Rebellion, the antiforeign movement in China in 1900. After Cixi died, Yuan was forced to retire. But when the 1911 revolution began, the dynasty asked him to return to command the army. In exchange, he was promised the premiership.

When the Manchu gave up the throne, Yuan became the first president of the Chinese Republic with headquarters in Peking (Beijing). At the same time Sun Yat-sen had set up a republic based on his ideas in Nanjing (Nanking) on the Yangtze River. To avoid a civil war, Sun agreed to allow Yuan to head the government.

Yuan steadily gained control and created a government made up of his friends and allies. On the threat of war with Japan, he gave in to Japanese demands to control much of China. Revolts erupted and Yuan's power shrank. He died in 1916.

Zhou Enlai or Chou En-lai (1898–1976): Zhou was one of China's most respected leaders. As a youth he took part in the May Fourth Movement and was imprisoned for his activism. After several months, he was released and went to France with a work-study group. While there, he joined the Communist Party in 1922. He set up several

European branches of the CCP. Zhou returned to China in 1924 and joined Sun Yat-sen's Kuomintang (KMT), or Nationalists, who had formed an alliance with the Communists. He was appointed deputy director of the political department of the Huangpu (Whampoa) Military Academy headed by Chiang Kai-shek. When Sun died in 1925, Chiang became the KMT leader and broke the alliance with the Communists, purging and killing many of them.

Zhou escaped, joining Mao and the Red Army in the Long March (1934–1935) to northwest China, where a Communist stronghold was set up. After the establishment of the People's Republic of China in 1949, Zhou became prime minister and foreign minister. He gave up the foreign ministry in 1958. He kept the premiership throughout Mao's reign and during the Cultural Revolution. After his death in 1976, thousands of Chinese gathered at Tiananmen Square on Qingming, a traditional festival for remembering the dead, to honor Zhou as a hero.

Zhu De or Chu Teh (1886–1976): Born in Sichuan, China, Zhu was one of thirteen children. Some sources say his father was a wealthy landlord. Others say his father was a poor peasant. The latter may be accurate, since an uncle adopted him when he was nine years old and paid for his education.

Zhu became a revolutionary and joined Sun Yat-sen's Kuomintang (KMT). He took part in the 1911 rebellion that helped topple the Qing dynasty. After Yuan Shikai came to power, Zhu and other KMT members went into exile. Zhu returned in 1916 and became a warlord. In 1922 he went to Paris and then Berlin, where he met Zhou Enlai. Zhou, by this time, had joined the Chinese Communist Party. Influenced by Zhou, Zhu also became a member of the CCP.

Back in China, Zhu, along with other Communists was purged from the KMT by Chiang Kai-shek. Zhu joined Mao Zedong's forces and became a commander in the Red Army. He was Mao's comrade-in-arms for many years and led a Red Army division out of Jiangxi Province during the Long March (1934–1935). When the Communists reached Yenan, Zhu was appointed supreme commander of the army, which by then was called the People's Liberation Army. After Mao and the PLA established the People's Republic of China, Zhu was chairman of the National People's Congress from 1959 to 1967.

In spite of his loyalty to Mao, Zhu was attacked by Red Guards during Mao's Cultural Revolution (1966–1976). After Zhu adopted Mao's ideas, he was brought back into the fold as China's head of state, although he had no power. He died in 1976.

Source Notes

p. 5   Quoted in Burton F. Beers, *World History Patterns of Civilization* (Englewood Cliffs, NJ: Prentice Hall, 1983), 517.

p. 9   Quoted in Roger Pelissier, *The Awakening of China 1793–1949,* ed. and trans. Martin Kieffer (New York: G.P. Putnam's Sons, 1966), 251.

p. 10–11   Theodore H. White and Annalee Jacoby, *Thunder out of China* (New York: W. Sloane Associates, 1946; repr., New York and Cambridge, MA: Da Capo Press, 1980), 21–22.

p. 12   Quoted in Pelissier, *Awakening of China,* 249.

p. 13   Quoted in Leonard H. D. Gordon, "Sun Yat-sen and His Legacy," *World and I,* September 1999, 328–41.

p. 15–16   Herbert A. Giles, *China and the Manchus* (Project Gutenberg Ebook, March 25, 2006), chap. 12, <http://www.gutenberg.org/files/2156/2156-h/2156-h.htm#2HCH0012> (accessed March 22, 2007).

p. 17   Quoted in Immanuel C.Y. Hsu, *The Rise of Modern China,* 4th ed. (New York and Oxford: Oxford University Press, 1990), 475.

p. 20   Quoted in Pelissier, *Awakening of China,* 259.

p. 23   Edwin John Dingle, *Across China on Foot* (Project Gutenberg Ebook #13420, September 10, 2004), chap. 1. <http://www.gutenberg.org/files/

13420/13420-h/13420-h.htm#CHAPTER_I> (accessed March 22, 2007).

p. 26   Quoted in Pelissier, *Awakening of China*, 259.

p. 27–28   Jonathan D. Spence, *The Search for Modern China* (New York: W.W. Norton & Company, 1990), 286.

p. 29   Edwin P. Hoyt, *The Rise of the Chinese Republic from the Late Emperor to Deng Xiaoping* (New York: McGraw-Hill, 1989), 44.

p. 32   W. Reginald Wheeler, *China and the World War* (New York: Macmillan, 1919), chap. 1, <http://www.lib.byu.edu/~rdh/wwi/comment/chinawwi/ChinaC1.htm> (accessed March 22, 2007); see also "Primary Documents: 'Twenty-One Demands' Made by Japan to China, 18 January 1915," <http://www.firstworldwar.com/source/21demands.htm> (accessed March 22, 2007).

p. 33   Spence, *The Search for Modern China*, 291.

p. 35–36   Quoted in Pelissier, *The Awakening of China*, 276.

p. 36   John King Fairbank and Merle Goldman, *China: A New History* (Cambridge, MA: Belknap Press of Harvard University Press, 2002), 173.

p. 37   Quoted in W. Scott Morton and Charlton M. Lewis, *China Its History and Culture*, 4th ed. (New York: McGraw-Hill, 2004), 184.

p. 38   Quoted in Richard R. Wertz, "The May 4th Movement," section a5 in "Rebellion and Revolution," in

Exploring Chinese History, <http://www.ibiblio.org/chinesehistory/contents/03pol/c02sa05.html> (accessed March 22, 2007).

p. 46   Quoted in Hoyt, *Rise of the Chinese Republic,* 82.

p. 47   Quoted in Jacques Guillermaz, *A History of the Chinese Communist Party 1921–1949,* trans. Anne Destenay (New York: Random House, 1972), 117.

p. 48–49   Zhou Enlai, "On Taking Prompt Punitive Action Against Chiang Kai-Shek," April 1927, in *Selected Works of Zhou En-lai,* vol. 1, Zhou Enlai Internet Archive, December 2001, <http://www.marxists.org/reference/archive/zhou-en-lai/1927/04/x01.htm> (accessed July 17, 2007).

p. 48   Guillermaz, *Chinese Communist Party 1921–1949,* 112.

p. 55   Mao Zedong, *Mao Tse-Tung: Selected Works* (New York: International Publishers, 1954), 1:23.

p. 56   Ibid., 80.

p. 57   Quoted in Edgar Snow, *Red Star Over China* rev. ed. (New York: Grove Press, 1968), p. 166.

p. 58   Quoted in Edgar Snow, *Red Star over China,* rev. ed. (New York: Grove Press, 1968), 174.

p. 58   Mao Tse-Tung, "On Guerrilla Warfare," in *Selected Works of Mao Tse-Tung,* vol. 9, 1937, Mao Tse-tung Reference Archive, <http://www.marxists.org/reference/archive/mao/works/1937/guerrilla-warfare/> (accessed October 11, 2007).

p. 62   Quoted in Pelissier, *Awakening of China,* 336.

p. 57 Snow, *Red Star over China*, 166.

p. 57 Edgar Snow, *Red Star over China*, 194.

p. 60 Quoted in Spence, *The Search for Modern China*, 415.

p. 64 Jung Chang and Jon Halliday, p. 153.

p. 64 Sun Shuyun, "Long March: The True Story behind a Myth," *Daily Yomiuri Online*, March 7, 2006, <http://www.yomiuri.co.jp/dy/columns/syndicate/20060615dy02.htm> (accessed March 22, 2007).

p. 65–66 Quoted in Hoyt, *Rise of the Chinese Republic*, 143.

p. 70–71 Quoted in Hoyt, *Rise of the Chinese Republic*, 156.

p. 72–73 Quoted in Hoyt, *Rise of the Chinese Republic*, 159.

p. 76 White and Jacoby, *Thunder out of China*, 52.

p. 76–78 Frank Tillman Durdin, "All Captives Slain," *New York Times*, December 18, 1937, 1, 10, in Paul Halsall, "Modern History Sourcebook: The Nanking Massacre, 1937," August 1997, <http://www.fordham.edu/halsall/mod/nanking.html> (accessed March 22, 2007). See also "The Nanking Atrocities," online documentary, 2000, <http://www.geocities.com/nankingatrocities/Fall/fall_01.htm> (accessed March 22, 2007); also "Nanking Massacre 1937," <http://prion.bchs.uh.edu/~zzhang/1/Nanking_Massacre/report.html> (accessed March 22, 2007).

p. 77 White and Jacoby, *Thunder out of China*, 54.

p. 78 Iris Chang, *The Rape of Nanking: The Forgotten Holocaust of World War II* (New York: Basic Books, 1997), 105–39.

p. 86 Roger Bilstein, "Flying the Hump," United States Army Air Forces in World War II, <http://www.usaaf.net/ww2/airlift/airliftpg7.htm> (accessed March 22, 2007).

p. 87–88 Robert L. Scott, *God Is My Co-Pilot* (New York: Ballantine Books, 1943), 132.

p. 88 Geoffrey Arend, "Air Cargo took off Above the Himalayas," *Air Cargo News,* June 6, 2006.

p. 88–89 Frank Moraes, *Report on Mao's China* (New York: Macmillan, 1954), 1–2.

p. 91 Fred C. Robins, arranged for publication by Ruby M. Robins, *Overseas Diary: India and Burma, World War II* (Gainesville, MO: Rumaro Press, 1990), 199.

p. 93 Quoted in Youth Division of Soka Gakkai, comp. *Cries for Peace: Experiences of Japanese Victims of World War II* (Tokyo: Japan Times, 1978), 129.

p. 94–95 Quoted in *Youth Division of Soka Gakkai,* Cries for Peace, 178–79.

p. 97 Zhou Enlai, "Actively Propagate Opposition to Civil War and Dictatorship and Expose Chiang Kai-Shek's Deceitful Plot," August 16, 1945, in *Selected Works of Zhou Enlai, vol. 1,* Zhou Enlai Internet Archive, December 2002, <http://www.marxists.org/reference/archive/zhou-enlai/1945/08/16.htm> (accessed July 17, 2007).

p. 97–98 *Mao Tse-Tung: Selected Works,* 5:47

p. 98 *Mao Tse-Tung: Selected Works,* 5:53. Also see: *Works of Mao Zedong by Date* <http://www.marxists.org/reference/archive/mao/selected-works/date-index.htm> (accessed March 22, 2007).

p. 102 *Mao Tse-Tung: Selected Works,* 5:418.

p. 104 Hsu, *The Rise of Modern China,* 643.

p. 105 Quoted in Pelissier, *Awakening of China,* 464.

p. 105 Ibid., 496.

p. 105 Hsu, *The Rise of Modern China,* 640.

p. 105 Edwin P. Hoyt, 212.

p. 106 Ibid., 143.

p. 107 Quoted in Roger Pellissier, 484.

p. 108 Theodore H. White and Annalee Jacoby, 140.

p. 108 Ibid., 143.

p. 108–109 Edgar Snow, *Red Star over China,* 279–80.

p. 110 Moraes, *Report on Mao's China,* 11.

p. 110 Patricia Buckley Ebrey, *The Cambridge Illustrated History of China* (New York: Cambridge University Press, 1996), 286.

p. 111 Guillermaz, *History of the Chinese Communist Party,* 442–44.

p. 113 White and Jacoby, *Thunder out of China*, 226–29.

p. 114 *Mao Tse-Tung: Selected Works*, 5:149.

p. 115 Mao Zedong, "The Chinese People Have Stood Up!" September 21, 1949, UCLA Center for East Asian Studies, East Asian Studies Documents, <http://www.isop.ucla.edu/eas/documents/mao490921.htm> (accessed March 22, 2007).

p. 116 Quoted in Rose Tang, "Revolution's Children: The Collapse of Ideology Leaves Generations Adrift in a Moral Vacuum," *Asiaweek*, September 24, 1999, <http://www.pathfinder.com/asiaweek/magazine/99/0924/cn_journeys.html#artist> (accessed October 21, 2007).

p. 117 Fairbank and Goldman, *China: A New History*, 339.

p. 118 Li Zhisui, *The Private Life of Chairman Mao: The Memoirs of Mao's Personal Physician*, trans. Tai Hung-chao (New York: Random House, 1994), 86.

p. 118 Deng Xiaoping, "Build Socialism with Chinese Characteristics," June 30, 1984, <http://www.wellesley.edu/Polisci/wj/China/Deng/Building.htm> (accessed October 10, 2007).

p. 118 Ibid.

p. 121 Quoted in Louisa Lim, "China's Students Changed by Tiananmen," BBC News, January 20, 2005, <http://news.

bbc.co.uk/2/hi/asia-pacific/4191129.stm> (accessed March 22, 2007).

p. 121 John Gittings, *The Changing Face of China: From Mao to Market* (Oxford and New York: Oxford University Press, 2005), 325.

Bibliography

Arend, Geoffrey. "Air Cargo Took Off above the Himalayas." *Air Cargo News,* June 6, 2006. <http://www.aircargonews. com/060606/humpstory.html> (accessed March 22, 2007).

Bilstein, Roger. "Flying the Hump." United States Army Air Forces in World War II. <http://www.usaaf.net/ww2/airlift/airliftpg7. htm> (accessed March 22, 2007).

Blum, John M., et al. *The National Experience,* 2nd ed. Part 2. New York: Harcourt, Brace, and World, 1968.

Chang, Iris. *The Rape of Nanking: The Forgotten Holocaust of World War II.* New York: Basic Books, 1997.

Ebeling, Richard M. "The Great Chinese Inflation." *Freeman,* December 2004. <http://www.fee.org/publications/the-freeman/ article.asp?aid=4584> (accessed March 22, 2007).

Ebrey, Patricia Buckley. *The Cambridge Illustrated History of China.* New York: Cambridge University Press, 1996.

Fairbank, John King, and Merle Goldman. *China: A New History.* Enlarged ed. Cambridge, MA and London: Belknap Press of Harvard University Press, 2002.

First World War.com. "Primary Documents: 'Twenty-One Demands' Made by Japan to China, 18 January 1915." <http://www.first worldwar.com/source/21demands.htm> (accessed March 22, 2007).

Giles, Herbert A. *China and the Manchus.* Chap. 12. First published 1912. Project Gutenberg Ebook, March 25, 2006. <http://www.gutenberg.org/files/2156/2156-h/2156-h.htm#2HCH0012> (accessed March 22, 2007).

Global Financial Data. "China Yuan Renminbi August 31, 1948–December 29, 2006. <http://www.globalfinancialdata.com/index.php3?action=detailedinfo&id=4005> (accessed March 22, 2007).

Gordon, Leonard H. D. "Sun Yat-sen and His Legacy." *World and I,* September 1999.

Guillermaz, Jacques. *A History of the Chinese Communist Party 1921–1949.* Translated by Anne Destenay. New York: Random House, 1972. Originally published 1968 in France.

Hoyt, Edwin P. *The Rise of the Chinese Republic: From the Last Emperor to Deng Xiaoping.* New York: McGraw-Hill, 1989.

Hsu, Immanuel C. Y. *The Rise of Modern China.* 4th ed. New York and Oxford: Oxford University Press, 1990.

Lim, Louisa. "China's Students Changed by Tiananmen." BBC News, January 20, 2005. <http://news.bbc.co.uk/2/hi/asia-pacific/4191129.stm> (accessed March 22, 2007).

Mao Zedong. "The Chinese People Have Stood Up!" September 21, 1949. UCLA Center for East Asian Studies, East Asian Studies Documents. <http://www.isop.ucla.edu/eas/documents/mao490921.htm> (accessed March 22, 2007).

———. "On Guerrilla Warfare." *In Selected Works of Mao Tse-Tung.* Vol. 9. 1937. Mao Tse-Tung Reference Archive. <http://www.

marxists.org/reference/archive/mao/works/1937/guerrilla-warfare/index.htm> (accessed March 22, 2007).

———. *Mao Tse-Tung: Selected Works*. Vols. 1–5. New York: International Publishers, 1954.

Morton, W. Scott, and Charlton M. Lewis. *China: Its History and Culture*. 4th ed. New York: McGraw-Hill, 2004.

Pelissier, Roger. *The Awakening of China 1793–1949*. Edited and translated by Martin Kieffer. New York: G.P. Putnam's Sons, 1966.

Roberts, J.A.G. *A Concise History of China*. Cambridge, MA: Harvard University Press, 1999.

Scott, Robert L. *God Is My Co-Pilot*. New York: Ballantine Books, 1943.

Sherry, Mark D. *China Defensive*. U.S. Army Center of Military History. Last updated October 3, 2003. <http://www.army.mil/cmh-pg/brochures/72-38/72-38.htm> (accessed March 22, 2007).

Spence, Jonathan D. *The Search for Modern China*. New York: W.W. Norton, 1990.

Time. "Crisis." November 13, 1944. <time/magazine/article/0,9171,801570,00.html> (accessed March 22, 2007).

———. "Generalissimo and Madame Chiang Kai-Shek." January 3, 1938. <http://www.time.com/time/subscriber/personofthe year/archive/stories/1937.html> (accessed March 22, 2007).

Wertz, Richard R. "The May 4th Movement." Section a5 of "Rebellion and Revolution." in *Exploring Chinese History*. <http://www.ibiblio.org/chinesehistory/contents/03pol/c02sa05.html> (accessed March 22, 2007).

Wheeler, W. Reginald. *China and the World War*. Chap. 1. <http://www.lib.byu.edu/~rdh/wwi/comment/chinawwi/ChinaC1.htm> (accessed March 22, 2007).

White, Theodore H. and Annalee Jacoby. *Thunder out of China*. New York: William Sloane Associates, 1946. Reprint of first edition. New York and Cambridge, MA: Da Capo Press, 1980.

Wolf, Mur. "Wellesley Person of the Week, Week of August 14, 2000: Madame Chiang Kai-shek."<http://www.wellesley.edu/Anniversary/chiang.html> (accessed March 22, 2007).

Youth Division of Soka Gakkai, comp. *Cries for Peace: Experiences of Japanese Victims of World War II*. Tokyo: Japan Times, 1978.

Zhou, Jinghao. "Keys to Women's Liberation in Communist China: An Historical Overview." *Journal of International Women's Studies*, November 2003.

For Further Reading and Websites

Books

Behnke, Alison. *China in Pictures.* Minneapolis: Twenty-First Century Books, 2003.

Chang, Iris. *The Rape of Nanking: The Forgotten Holocaust of World War II.* New York: Penguin, 1998.

Chen, Da. *China's Son: Growing Up in the Cultural Revolution.* New York: Random House, 2003.

Gay, Kathlyn. *Mao Zedong's China.* Minneapolis: Twenty-First Century Books, 2008.

Malaspina, Ann. *The Chinese Revolution and Mao Zedong in World History.* Berkeley Heights, NJ: Enslow, 2004.

Morton, W. Scott, and Charlton M. Lewis. *China: Its History and Culture.* 4th ed. New York: McGraw-Hill, 2004.

Scott, Robert L. *God Is My Co-Pilot.* New York: Ballantine Books, 1943.

Stewart, Whitney. *Mao Zedong.* Minneapolis: Twenty-First Century Books, 2006.

White, Theodore H., and Analee Jacoby. *Thunder out of China.* New York: William Sloane Associates, 1946. Reprint of first edition. New York and Cambridge, MA: Da Capo Press, 1980.

Wong, Jan. *Red China Blues: My Long March from Mao to Now.* New York: Anchor Books, 1997.

WEBSITES

Chiang Kai-shek
<http://www.bartleby.com/65/ch/ChiangKa.html>
This site contains a Columbia Encyclopedia entry on the Nationalist
  leader Chiang Kai-shek.

Madame Chiang Kai-shek
<http://www.wellesley.edu/Anniversary/chiang.html>
Madame Chiang was a graduate of Wellesley University in Massachu-
  setts, and an article about her as Wellesley's Person of the Week
  is on the site.

Modern China 1911 Revolution
<http://www.wsu.edu:8080/~dee/MODCHINA/REV.HTM>
This site includes a good summary of the 1911 Revolution by Richard Hooker.

Qing Dynasty
<http://www.mnsu.edu/emuseum/prehistory/china/later_imperial_
  china/qing.html>
On this site, the Qing dynasty is described in an article about the
  Manchu. A map of the area the emperors ruled is also included.

Index

Across China on Foot (Dingle), 23
agriculture: under Deng, 119; land reform under Communists, 102–103, 112; under Manchus, 10; under Mao, 117; protests against landowners, 43; during World War II, 93
Allies, 83, 84
Altar of Heaven, 26
armies: National Protection Army, 28; National Revolutionary Army (Nationalist Army), 40, 42, 50–51, 60; New Army, 4–5, 7, 8; strikes and foreign, 45; of warlords, 29, 42, 50–51, 68; and Yuan (Beiyang Army), 20–21, 22. *See also* KMT Army; Red Army
atomic bombs, 94–96
Austria, 6, 31
Autumn Harvest Uprising, 55–56
Axis, 83

Beijing: as capital under Yuan, 21; captured by Japanese, 76; KMT control, 51; National Shame Day, 36–38; protests against People's Republic, 120–121; Temple of Heaven, 26–27
Beijing National University, 36–38
Beiyang Army, 20–21, 22
Belden, Jack, 107–108
Big Four Families, 105–106, 115
Blue Shirts, 60
Borodin, Michael, 40
Braun, Otto, 61, 63
Bulgaria, 31

Burma, 86, 91, 92
Burma Road, 86, 87, 91

Cambridge Illustrated History of China, The (Ebrey), 110
Canton. *See* Guangzhou
Central Powers, 31
Chang, Iris, 78
Chiang Kai-shek: campaigns against Red Army, 59–61, 62, 68; as cause of Nationalist loss, 110–115; criticism of, 105; death, 115; and Huangpu Military Academy, 42; and Japanese aggression, 68; kidnapped, 70–73; Mao's call for overthrow of, 114–115; marriage, 50; New Life Movement, 60; Northern Expedition, 42; popularity of, 52; pre-World War II relations with CCP, 45–48; and Stalin, 72; and Stilwell, 89–92; and Sun, 40; on Taiwan, 115; 228 Incident, 114; and U.S., 84–85, 89–92
China-Burma-India (CBI) Mission, 86–92
Chinese Communist Party (CCP): alliances with KMT, 40, 42, 73–75, 80–82; basic policies, 114–115; Cultural Revolution, 117–118; and Deng, 118–119, 120; ideals, 111–112; influence of USSR, 53–54, 56; and Japanese surrender, 97; life of leaders, 113; and peasants, 42, 53–54, 55–56, 101, 102–103; post-World War II KMT offensives against, 98–100; post-World War II negotiations with

KMT, 98; pre-World War II relations with Chiang, 45–48; protests against, 120–121; reasons for victory of, 110–115; rise to power of Mao in, 112, 113–116; and Shanghai strikes, 45; and Sun, 39–40, 42; and women, 35, 102–103

Chinese National Airways Corporation, 52

Chongqing, 80

Christian General, 31

Chu Teh, 113

City of Five Goats, 10

Cixi (Empress Dowager), 18, 20

Comintern, 40

Confucian ideology, 24, 34–35

corruption: after Second Revolution, 25; and CCP, 115; and Nationalists, 93, 104–106; and warlords, 30; and Yuan, 22

Cultural Revolution (1966-1976), 117–118

currency, 106

Dadu River crossing, 64

democracy: and government of Chiang, 110; Republic of China declared, 15; support for, 28

Democratic League, 100

Deng Xiaoping, 118–121

Dewey, John, 38

Dingle, Edwin, 23

diseases, 108

divorce, 103

doomed men, 108

Durdin, Frank Tillman, 76–78

Ebrey, Patricia Buckley, 110

Echo Wall, 27

economy: under Deng, 118–119; Five-Power Banking Consortium loan, 22; importance of Shanghai, 21;

of Manchuria, 31–32, 67; under Manchus, 7; under Mao, 117; under Republic of China, 105–106; and Turkey, 31

education, 52, 79, 119

Empress Dowager, 18, 20

England. *See* Great Britain

Enola Gay, 94

extraterritoriality, 5, 16

Fairbank, John King, 35, 114

famine, 93

farming: under Deng, 119; land reform under Communists, 102–103, 112; under Manchus, 10; under Mao, 117; protests against landowners, 43; during World War II, 93

fascism, 60

Feng Yuxiang, 31, 42

First United Front, 42, 48-49

Five-Power Banking Consortium, 22

Flying Tigers, 86–89

Flying Typers, 88

foot binding, 34, 35

Four Modernizations, 118

France: Five-Power Banking Consortium, 22; sphere of influence, 5; World War I, 31, 33, 34

gambling, 6

gangsters, 47

Germany: aid to Chiang, 60; Five-Power Banking Consortium, 22; sphere of influence, 6; territory in China, 34–35; World War I, 31; World War II, 83, 92

Gittings, John, 121

God Is My Co-Pilot (Scott), 87–88

golden lilies, 34

gold yuan (currency), 106

Great Britain: Five-Power Banking Consortium, 22; Hong Kong given to, 5; and May 30th Movement, 44; Opium War, 5, 17; seizure of Guangzhou, 17; sphere of influence, 5; Sun imprisoned in, 13; and Twenty-One Demands, 32–33; World War I, 31, 33, 34; World War II, 83, 96

Great Proletarian Cultural Revolution (1966-1976), 117–118

Great Snow mountain range, 65

Green Gang, 47

Guadalcanal, 92

Guangdong Province, 32

Guangzhou: background of, 32; failed attempt by Sun to seize, 12; Huangpu Military Academy in, 40; May 30th Movement, 44; Nationalist Revolution, 9; population, 36; seized by Great Britain, 17; Sun in, 39

Guardian (British newspaper), 121

guerrilla tactics: ineffective against Japanese, 81; as military strategy of Mao, 58–59, 63; Red Army training in, 58; success against KMT Army, 102

Guillermaz, Jacques, 111

Halliday, Jon, 64

Han Chinese, 12

Hankou, 8, 78

Hanyang, 8

Harris, Nigel, 46

Himalayas, 86

Hiroshima, Japan, 94–95

homes of peasants, 10–11

Hong Kong: given to British, 5; strikes, 44, 47

Hoyt, Edwin P., 29, 106

Hsu, C.Y., 104, 106

Huangpu Military Academy, 40, 42, 60

Hubei Province, 31

The Hump, 86–89

Hunan Province, 31

infanticide, 6

Italy: sphere of influence, 5; World War I, 31, 34; World War II, 83

Iwo Jima, 92

Jacoby, Annalee: on Japanese strategy, 78–79; on KMT soldiers, 107, 108; on peasant homes and villages, 10–11

Japan: Five-Power Banking Consortium, 22; in Manchuria, 31–33, 67; sphere of influence, 5; and Taiwan, 114, 115; Twenty-One Demands, 32–33, 36; World War I, 31; World War II, 83, 86–96, 97

Japan, war with: alliance between CCP and KMT, 73–75; and Chiang, 68; cities captured by Japanese, 76–78; civil war during, 68, 70, 73, 81; incident beginning, 74; population relocation during, 79–80; seizure of Manchuria, 67

Jiangxi Province, 59, 61

Jinggang mountains, 56

Jung Chang, 64

kamikaze attacks, 92

King Palace of Taiping Heavenly Kingdom, 20

KMT Army: capture of Mao, 57; leadership, 106; and Long March, 62; offensives against CCP after World War II, 98–100; resistance after People's Republic declared, 116; on Taiwan, 115; training, 85, 92; treatment of soldiers, 107–108; during World War II, 84–86

Kong family, 50

Kunming, 87, 88

Kuomintang (KMT): alliances with

CCP, 40, 42, 73–75, 80–82; Autumn Harvest Uprising, 55–56; capital, 50; factions, 53; as official government of China, 51; post-World War II negotiations with CCP, 98; and Song, 21; on Taiwan, 115; and Yuan, 22, 24. *See also* KMT Army; National Revolutionary Army (Nationalist Army)

labor unions, 44–45
land reform, 102–103, 112
Liberated Areas, 98, 99
Li Zhisui, 118
London, England, 13
London Globe (newspaper), 13
Long March, 61–66
Luding Bridge, 64
Lugou Bridge, 75

MacArthur, Douglas, 97
Madame Chiang Kai-shek: and kidnapping of Chiang, 72–73; marriage, 50; and Stilwell, 90
Madame Sun Yat-sen, 105
Manchu government: background of, 5–7, 12; grievances against, 5–7, 16; and Han Chinese, 24; protests against, 4–5; revolution against, 8–9; and Yuan, 18, 20
Manchukuo, 67
Manchuria: economic control of, 31–32; land reform under Communists, 102; seized by Japan, 67; Soviets in, 92; Twenty-One Demands, 32–33; warlords, 31
Mandate of Heaven (Harris), 46
Mao Zedong: Autumn Harvest Uprising, 54–56; on continuing to fight KMT after Japanese surrender, 97–99; and Cultural Revolution, 117–118; death, 116, 118; escape from KMT troops,

57; focus on peasants, 55; guerrilla tactics, 58–59, 63; increase in power, 63, 65; Long March, 63, 66; rise to power, 112, 113–114; training of Red Army, 57–59; vision of New China, 101–102
Marco Polo Bridge, 75
Marshall, George C., 100
May Fourth Movement, 36–38
May 30th Movement, 43–44
Ming Tomb, 20
mobsters, 47
modernization, 52
Mongolia, 32
Moraes, Frank, 88–89, 110

Nagasaki, Japan, 96
Nanjing: captured by Japanese, 76–78; historic buildings in, 20; as Nationalist capital, 8, 50
Nanking. *See* Nanjing
Nationalist/Nanjing decade, 51
Nationalist Party. *See* Kuomintang (KMT)
Nationalist Revolution: beginning of, 8; length of, 7
National Revolutionary Alliance, 13, 21
National Revolutionary Army (Nationalist Army): Chiang as generalissimo, 40, 50–51; Northern Expedition, 42; training academy, 40, 42, 43, 60. *See also* KMT Army
National Shame Day, 36–38
New Army: early victories, 8; Manchu discovery of, 4–5; and revolution, 7
New China, 101–102, 116
New Fourth Army Incident, 82
New Life Movement, 60
New York Times (newspaper), 76–78
Northern Expedition, 42
nuclear bombs, 94–96

Old Marshal, 31
opium addiction, 5, 17, 73
Opium War (1839-1842), 5, 17

Pagoda for Buddhist Relics, 20
Peasant Movement Training Institute, 55
peasants: and CCP, 40, 42, 53–54, 55–56, 101, 102–103, 112; famine of 1943, 93; living conditions, 10–11; and Long March, 61, 62; under Manchus, 9, 10; under Nationalists, 103–104; percent of population, 10; and Second Revolution, 24; under warlords, 30
People's Democracy, 14, 15
People's Liberation Army (PLA), 102. *See also* Red Army
People's Livelihood, 13, 14
People's Nationalism, 13, 14
People's Republic of China: under Deng, 118–121; established, 102, 115; hopes for, 117; KMT Army resistance after declaration of, 116; under Mao, 117–118; protests against, 120–121; and Taiwan, 9
Philippines, 92
Philosopher Marshal, 31
population: in early 1900s, 5; of Guangzhou, 36; migration during war with Japan, 79–80; peasants as percent of, 10
Potsdam Declaration, 94
protests: Autumn Harvest Uprising, 55–56; against Japanese, 44; against landowners, 44; against Manchus, 4–5; against People's Republic, 120–121; strikes by workers, 44; on Taiwan, 114; against World War I settlement, 36; against Yuan as emperor, 28

provinces: controlled by KMT, 50; controlled by warlords, 29, 31; independence, 8–9
Puyi (last emperor), 18, 20

Qing dynasty: end of rule, 21; and Han Chinese, 12; New Army and, 7; Opium War and unequal treaties, 17. *See also* Manchu government
queues (hairstyle), 12

railroads: nationalization by Manchus, 4; seized by Japan, 31
Rape of Nanking, 76–78
Rape of Nanking, The (Chang), 78
Red Army: and Autumn Harvest Uprising, 55–56; basic policies, 114–115; campaigns by Chiang against, 59–61, 62, 68; guerrilla tactics, 58–59, 63; life of soldiers, 108–109; Long March, 61–66; organized, 56; as part of Nationalist Army, 74, 82; renamed People's Liberation Army, 102; and Stilwell, 89, 91; training of soldiers, 57–59
Red Guard, 117
Red Star over China (Snow), 108–109
regents/regency, 20
Reinsch, Paul S., 35–36
Republic of China: criticism of, 105; declared democracy, 15; economy, 105–106; government corruption, 104–105; and peasants, 103–104; under Sun, 15–18; support for, 28; and Taiwan, 9; under Yuan, 21. *See also* Chiang Kai-shek
Revive China Society, 12
Robins, Fred C., 91
Roosevelt, Franklin D., 83, 91–92, 94
Rottach, Edmond, 12
Ruijin, 59

Russia: Five-Power Banking Consortium, 22; and Manchuria, 31–32; sphere of influence, 5. *See also* Union of Soviet Socialist Republics (USSR)

Safety Zone in Nanjing, 78
Salisbury, Lord, 13
Scott, Robert, 87–88
Second Revolution, 24-25
Second United Front, 73–75, 80–82
Seeckt, Hans von, 60
Shaanxi Province, 66, 73, 112
Shandong Province, 31, 35
Shanghai: in 1909, 13; captured by Japanese, 76; general strike, 44–46; importance of, 21; Nationalist Revolution, 9; political prisoners in, 73; protests against Japanese, 44
Snow, Edgar: on Dadu River crossing, 64; on escape of Mao from KMT troops, 57; on Red Army soldiers, 108–109
socialism, 14
social problems, 5–6, 105–106
Society for Comrades for Resistance Against Japan, 70
Solomon Islands, 92
Song Jiaoren, 21Son of Heaven, 26
Soong family, 50
Soong Meiling. *See* Madame Chiang Kai-shek
Soviet Union. *See* Union of Soviet Socialist Republics (USSR)
Spence, Jonathan D., 27–28, 33
spheres of influence, 5, 17
Stalin, Joseph, 72, 94
Stilwell, Joseph W., 89–92
strikes: general, 43–47; in Hong Kong, 46; against Japanese textile factories, 44
Stuart, John L., 105
Sun Shuyun, 64

Sun Yat-sen: beliefs, 13, 14–15; and Communists, 39–40, 42; death, 42; education, 9–10; exile, 13; Mausoleum, 20; and May Fourth Movement, 38; and National Revolutionary Alliance, 13; as president of Republic of China, 15–18; on weakness of imperial China, 6; and Yuan, 22–24

Taipei, 115
Taiwan: under Chiang, 114, 115; and People's Republic of China, 9; 228 Incident, 114
Tang dynasty tombs, 20
Tanno, Kiyoharu, 92–94
Tatu River crossing, 64
taxes: under Deng, 119; imposed by foreign governments on imports, 5, 17; under Manchus, 10; under Nationalists, 93, 105
Temple of Heaven, 26–27
Teng Jimeng, 121
territory controlled by foreign governments, 6, 17
theatrical productions, 9
Three People's Principles, 13–14
Tiananmen Square, Beijing, 37–38, 120–121
Tian Tan (Temple of Heaven), 26–27
Tombs of Southern Tang Emperors, 20
tourism, 20
trade: in Manchuria, 31–32, 67; and Manchus, 5; and taxes imposed by foreign governments, 5, 17; and Twenty-One Demands, 32–33
transportation, 52
Treaty of Nanjing, 5, 17
Truman, Harry S., 94, 100
Turkey, 31
Twenty-One Demands, 32–33, 36
228 Incident, 114

unequal treaties, 5, 17
Union of Soviet Socialist Republics (USSR): and CCP, 53–54, 56; Comintern, 40; as model, 56; and Shanghai strikes, 44; and Sun, 39–40, 41; World War II, 83, 92, 94. *See also* Russia
United States: and Chiang, 84–85, 86–92; recognition of Yuan government, 21; and Twenty-One Demands, 32–33; World War I, 31, 35–36. *See also* World War II
USS Missouri, 96

villages, 10–11, 22
Vinegar Joe, 86–92

warlords: background of, 29; campaigns against Red Army, 68; government under, 29; National Revolutionary Army assaults on, 43, 50–51; power in 1921 of, 39; power in 1927 of, 50; provinces controlled by, 29, 30, 31
Wedemeyer, Albert C., 92
Whampoa Military Academy. *See* Huangpu Military Academy
White, Theodore H.: on famine of 1943, 93; on Japanese strategy, 78–79; on KMT soldiers, 107, 108; on life of CCP party leaders, 113; on peasant homes and villages, 10–11; on population relocation during war with Japan, 79
White Army. *See* KMT Army
Wilson, Woodrow, 34

women: and Communists, 35, 102–103; in Confucian society, 34–35
World War I, 31–36
World War II: battles in Pacific, 92; beginning of, 83; China-Burma-India Mission, 86–92; famine during, 93; German surrender, 92; Japanese surrender, 96, 97; U.S. entrance, 83–84; U.S. support of KMT Army, 84–85
Wuchang, 4, 7
Wuhan, 78
Wu Peifu, 31, 42

Xuzhou, 50

Yan'an. *See* Yenan
Yang Hucheng, 68, 70–73
Yenan, 66, 112
yuan (currency), 106
Yuan Shikai: attempts to be emperor, 25–28; China under, 21–24; death, 29; and KMT, 22, 24; rise to power, 18, 20–21

Zhang Guotao, 66
Zhang Xueliang, 68, 70–73
Zhang Zoulin, 31, 42, 50
Zhao Youping, 116
Zhou Enlai: distrust of Chiang, 48, 97; and general strike, 45; and Huangpu Military Academy, 43; and New Fourth Army, 82; and Red Army breakout from Jiangxi, 61
Zhu De, 56, 57–59, 113
Zunyi, 63

Photo Acknowledgments

The images in this book are used with permission of: © Bettmann/ Corbis, 6, 11, 14, 19, 37, 43, 51, 54, 74, 77, 79, 87, 95, 99, 103, 107, 119, 120; Getty Images, 22; © Imagemore Co., Ltd./Corbis, 27; Steve Zmina, 30, 63; Underwood & Underwood/Corbis, 35; The Art Archive/Private Collection/Marc Charmet, 41; AFP/Getty Images, 45; © Hulton-Deutsch Collection/Corbis, 59, 71, 76, 85, 111; Hulton Archive/Getty Images, 65, 69; Time & Life Pictures/ Getty Images, 90, 104; AP Images, 81; © Yevgeny Khaldei/Corbis, 96; © Corbis, 112.

Front cover: © Topical Press Agency/Getty Images.

About the Author

Kathlyn Gay is the author of more than 120 books, some written in collaboration with family members who are scattered from coast to coast. Her books focus on social and environmental issues, culture, history, health, communication, and sports. Her other publications range from "first readers" and science booklets to young adult and adult nonfiction as well as encyclopedias, teacher manuals, and portions of textbooks. She has written hundreds of magazine features and stories. She lives in New Port Richey, Florida.